COPING WITH ALCOHOL

COPING WITH

Alcohol

Gail Gleason Milgram, Ed.D.

Illustrated by
Nancy Lou Gahan

THE ROSEN PUBLISHING GROUP, INC./
NEW YORK

Published in 1980, 1983, 1985, 1 9 8 7 by The Rosen Publishing Group
29 East 21st Street, New York, N.Y. 10010

Copyright 1980, 1983, 1985, 1987 by Gail G. Milgram

Revised Edition 1987

Library of Congress Cataloging in Publication Data

Milgram, Gail Gleason.
  Coping with alcohol.

  Bibliography: p. 119
  Includes index.
  1. Alcoholism. I. Title.
RC565.M443 1980.7   616.8'61   79–25817
ISBN 0–8239–0747–3

Manufactured in the United States of America

To my husband, Bill Milgram, who encourages growth, stimulates the accepting of challenges, and motivates the expansion of our worlds for Lynn, Anne, and me.

About the Author

Dr. Gail Gleason Milgram is a Professor and Director of Education and Training at the Center of Alcohol Studies, Rutgers University, New Brunswick, New Jersey. Alcohol use in American society, adolescent issues and concerns and patterns of youthful drinking and drug use, and alcohol/drug education have been major themes of her academic and professional endeavors. Her publications for the Richards Rosen Group highlight these topics: *The Teenager and Alcohol*, 1970; *The Teenager and Smoking*, 1972; and *The Teenager and Sex*, 1974. Other related publications include *Alcohol Education Materials: An Annotated Bibliography* and *What Is Alcohol and Why Do People Drink?* both published by the Rutgers Center of Alcohol Studies in 1975. *Your Future in Education,* published by the Richards Rosen Press in 1976, provided both a general and specific perspective on education. *What, When and How to Talk to Children About Alcohol and Other Drugs: A Guide for Parents* was published by Hazelden in 1983, and *What, When and How to Talk to Students About Alcohol and other Drugs: A Guide for Teachers,* co-authored with Thomas Griffin, was published by Hazelden in 1986.

Dr. Milgram's activities include presenting alcohol education workshops for educators, parents, college and high school students, and industrial personnel. She also teaches a graduate course entitled, "Social Implications of Alcohol Use in American Society." Though the many groups she deals with have diverse backgrounds and levels of education, their misinformation on alcohol facts and ambivalence toward alcohol use is a common factor. *Coping with Alcohol* was written to provide accurate information on alcohol and alcoholism and to motivate individuals to clarify their values related to alcohol use and misuse. The text has been revised and updated to reflect the most current information and to foster responsible decision-making regarding the use or nonuse of alcohol. A chapter on drugs in American society and adolescent drug use has been added to provide perspective and to heighten awareness of this relevant issue of the 1980s.

A native of New Jersey, Dr. Milgram holds a B.S. degree from Georgian Court College, Lakewood, New Jersey, and an M.Ed. and Ed.D. from Rutgers University. She is a member of many educational associations and professional groups and is listed in *Contemporary Authors, Who's Who of American Women,* and *World's Who's Who of Authors.* In private life, she is the wife of William H. Milgram and the mother of two daughters, Lynn Patricia and Anne Melissa.

Acknowledgments

A special note of thanks is extended to my husband and my family for their love, guidance, support, and confidence throughout the preparation of this text and always.

The author wishes to thank the following for their kind permission to quote from works held in copyright:

Cahalan, D. "Epidemiology: Alcohol Use in American Society." In Gomberg, E., White, H. and Carpenter, J.A. eds., *Alcohol, Science and Society Revisited.* New Brunswick, NJ: Rutgers Center of Alcohol Studies, 1982.

Milgram, G.G. "A Value Game: Drugs and Alcohol." American Youth. Ceco Publishing Company, 1979.

Milgram, G.G., *What Is Alcohol and Why Do People Drink?* New Brunswick, New Jersey: Rutgers Center of Alcohol Studies, 1975.

Lender, M. and Karnchanapee, K. "Temperance Tales" and the Alcoholic: Creation of a Stereotype." An Educational Slide Sound Film on the History of Alcohol Problems. New Brunswick, New Jersey: Rutgers Center of Alcohol Studies, 1979.

Contents

Introduction

Alcohol is a socially acceptable, legal drug that is consumed by the majority of Americans without creating problems for themselves or others. However, the United States is an unsure and ambivalent society regarding the use of alcoholic beverages. For example, an adult might feel that he has to have a drink at a business lunch, yet the same person would not feel pressure to have a dessert. Others in society worry about the phenomenon of teenage drinking, not remembering that their teen-ager was introduced to alcohol use at home. Still others believe that to "drink like a man" or be able to "hold your liquor" is a sign of masculinity and virility, forgetting or never having known that alcohol is a drug. These mixed emotions and lack of accurate information about alcohol often result in high-risk drinking, pressure to drink, and the covering up of problem drinkers or alcoholics by their loved ones.

Ironically, drinkers and nondrinkers alike are usually unaware of their misinformation and ambivalent feelings and attitudes. Society attempts to muddle through without learning more about or examining attitudes related to the use and abuse of alcohol. This is understandable when one considers the history of alcohol use in U.S. It has had extreme highs and lows: Prohibition, Repeal. These periods greatly influenced alcohol education. During

Prohibition and the time leading up to it, educators knew that the dangers and evils of alcohol should be stressed. The ultimate goal of this process was to produce a society of nondrinkers. Though people continued to drink during Prohibition, this fact was ignored in the classroom, where worms were dropped into 100 percent alcohol to stress visually the harm that could result from drinking. The fact that no one drinks 100 percent alcohol or that our stomachs are not made up of worms bothered no one but the students. As students listened to what society was teaching, they observed what society was drinking. Though this was not the origin of "Do as I say, not as I do," it serves as a classic example of this philosophy.

Alcohol education fared no better with Repeal. By this time no one was sure what should be taught about alcohol, but somehow mystically believed that abstinence should be the goal of education. By 1950 educators and concerned citizens were beginning to state that teen-agers needed honest, accurate, and objective information about alcohol. Unfortunately, most people were not listening, and what little alcohol education there was still frequently stressed the evils-and-dangers approach and hoped for an abstinent society. The inconsistency of this is clearly apparent when one realizes that studies of teen-age drinking in the 1950's indicated that approximately 70 percent of the teen-age population consumed alcohol and considered themselves "drinkers." This is similar to the statistics available for the 1980's.

Most adults of today experienced alcohol education that was either nonexistent, shrouded in mystery and irrelevancy, or a response to the emotionality of the times. They, as well as teen-agers, seem to lack a language for discussing alcohol use. The word "drinker" is most often interpreted to mean problem drinker, heavy drinker, alcoholic drinker, excessive drinker, abusive drinker. Drinker, in fact, means one who consumes a beverage; it is ironic that this word when it is associated with alcohol becomes a negative. The negative connotation is probably the reason that adults have trouble with the issue of teen-age drinking. Instead of considering this drinking as consumption of alcoholic beverages that may or may not result in problems, it is translated immediately into a problem activity. It is no wonder that teen-agers today seem as ambivalent and as reluctant to discuss their use of, feelings toward, and attitudes about alcohol as are their parents.

The lack of understood language and definition of alcohol terms is also apparent when the words used to describe an intoxicated person are listed: drunk, high, tight, tipsy, smashed, blotto, stoned. A communication problem also surrounds the terms problem drinker, abusive drinker, and alcoholic. These definitional problems are further exaggerated in the issue of teen-age drinking. Is a teen-ager who is high a problem drinker? Does a teen-ager have a problem related to his/her use of alcohol, or does that teen-ager have an alcohol problem? They are not the same. A teen-ager may have come home intoxicated one evening and gotten into trouble with her parents, which resulted in her being grounded for a month. This is a problem related to alcohol use, but not an alcohol problem. On the other hand, a teen-ager may be secretly drinking alcohol continually throughout the day to cope with life; this is an alcohol problem. Unfortunately, society often lumps the two types of problems into one and comes up with a teen-age problem-drinking, pre-alcoholic, or alcoholic population. This further clouds our ability to communicate, as adults seem too quick to label activities of teen-agers as problems and teen-agers choose not to open up about their reality for fear of being labeled a problem.

Another topic of concern has further hindered communication between adults and teen-agers: the drug era. Interestingly alcohol, though a drug, was not part of the country's concern over drug usage by the adolescent population. Reading the newspapers and periodicals of the 1960's, it would appear that teen-agers had stopped drinking and switched to other mood-modifying substances. Reading about teen-age behavior in the 1970's would lead one to believe that they had dropped other drugs and were using alcohol exclusively. There is little truth to these one-sided characterizations. Alcohol was in the 1960's, is in the 1980's, and probably will be in the 1990's the drug of choice for most teen-agers. In the late 1980's teen-age alcohol problems and the growing use of "crack" seem to be characterizing the youthful population and to be vying for society's attention as the issue of the day. Nor have other "hard" and "soft" drugs disappeared. The serious effects of these drugs have not changed, nor has the danger in mixing them with alcohol; they are merely not being emphasized in the media, except for "crack." The media tend to stress what society wants stressed, and the current topic of greatest concern seems to be teen-age alcohol problems. Though the group of teen-agers experiencing problem drinking did not appear overnight, they have become a favorite subject of public and private discussion. Adults have been reacting to teen-age drinking as if they were watching a tennis match: "Thank God he's only drinking (and not taking drugs)" and "The numbers of teen-age alcoholics are overwhelming." The ambivalence in these statements was not created by the media, but rather is another example of our lack of ability to deal with alcohol, the drug.

The effects of our society's ambivalence and uncertainties about alcohol are as real today as they were during Prohibition and Repeal. Alcohol education is not a national priority in the U.S. In fact, its existence and goals vary not only from state to state but often from school to school in the same district. Teachers have often been made to feel uncomfortable in covering this topic and are unsure of the desired goal. Is it abstinence for life? Abstinence till the legal drinking age? Responsible drinking? Parents are also insecure: Though alcohol education is acknowledged to be important, it becomes controversial if you're teaching my nondrinking child that some use of alcohol is appropriate. This parallels the fear of parents regarding sex education. If you discuss it, "they" might try it. On the opposite side, parents who are drinkers may not be comfortable with their child's learning that drinking is dangerous. Children representing both extreme positions are in the class, as well as children of alcoholic parents. The dilemma of alcohol education and its goals is obvious.

To circumvent this problem and still cover alcohol, society's solution has been devious at best. The following assumptions have been offered as rationale for learning about alcohol. These assumptions are related to grade level in school and reality for ease of understanding.

Grade Level: K-6. No alcohol education.

Assumption: Young people don't drink, so they don't need alcohol education in elementary school.

Reality: Young people observe drinking that takes place around them and have questions related to alcohol use. Also, many children are introduced to alcohol in the home between the ages of 11 and 13 and have direct questions about its use.

Questions: What is alcohol? Why do people drink? Do people drink differently? Why do some people not drink?

Grade Level: Junior High. Alcoholism education.

Assumption: If the problems related to use of any substance are stressed, the person will choose not to use the substance.

Reality: The junior high student may have already been given a drink by his parents.*

Questions: What are the various beverages? How are they made and are they different? What are the effects of alcohol on the body? How much can I drink?

Grade Level: High School. Alcohol education.

Assumption: Teen-agers are close to the legal drinking age and therefore should learn about alcoholic beverages and their effects on the human body.

Reality: Many teen-agers have been consuming alcohol and have learned through experimentation some information on the beverages and their effects on the human body.

Questions: What are the warning signs of problem drinking? What is the disease of alcoholism? Can it be treated?

Teen-agers might well ask why they should learn about alcohol if the adult population in society survives with misinformation, myths, and ambivalence. Society's only hope for lowering risks related to alcohol use and reducing the problem-drinking and alcoholic populations is dissemination of accurate information about alcohol use. Though education may not prevent alcohol prob-

---

* Many adults and parents don't realize that the effects of alcohol on the human body are directly related to the body's weight. If an 80 lb. adolescent is given one-half a normal size drink, it is as if the individual was given a whole drink.

lems, it will produce a population knowledgeable about the drug, alcohol, which they consume and enable earlier identification of persons who are having alcohol problems. Another hopeful result would be to eliminate the stigma often attached to the disease of alcoholism, the alcoholic, and the family of the alcoholic.

Alcohol education is no longer limited to the adolescent population. Nor can it be. It is occurring on college campuses, in community groups, for specific target populations (such as parents of young children), and in industry awareness programs. Yet it must also be part of the educational process for teen-agers.

The following are the most important reasons for you to learn about alcohol:

1. Alcoholic beverages have played a major role in the history of our country and of other countries also.
2. Alcohol is a part of our society. Whether people drink alcoholic beverages or not, they are still exposed to the use of alcohol.
3. Alcoholic beverages are consumed by a large number of people in our country. At least two-thirds of the adults in the U.S. drink alcoholic beverages at some time during a year.
4. Approximately 70 percent of the teen-agers in the U.S. drink alcoholic beverages. If you are one who drinks, you should know what you are drinking, why you are drinking, and the effects of alcohol on you. If you are one who does not drink, you should understand and clarify your feelings about why you do not drink and also know what it is that others drink.
5. It is important that you understand how your family feels about alcohol. Knowing why they do or do not drink will help you understand their feelings.

6. The U.S. is made up of peoples from many lands; the customs and habits of each group are called their culture. Many cultures mix in the U.S. to form our society. Even though the cultures mix, each person maintains a cultural background that influences the way he/she feels about alcohol use, drinking patterns, and attitudes toward drinking. Some people who drink have problems with alcohol and may have an illness called alcoholism.

7. It is estimated that there are over six million alcoholics in the U.S. and some four million problem drinkers. Many other people have problems because of their alcohol use or the alcohol use of a loved one. One of you may have a parent with a drinking problem. Though information about alcohol will not solve that problem, it will help you to understand it, and it may motivate you to talk it over with someone. Most important, the information should help you to realize that you are not the cause of the problem nor will you be able to solve your parent's problem.

8. Adolescents have questions about alcohol and its use. For example: What is it? How is it used? Why do people drink? Why is it legal? What are alcohol problems?

Many young people find it hard to ask about alcohol. They are sometimes puzzled about who should be asked and when; therefore many important questions are asked of friends who probably do not have all the right answers. You might find that your parents and teachers will welcome questions and will answer them honestly. Adults often are more at ease in answering questions than they are in bringing up a topic.

You probably have more of your own reasons why young people should learn about alcohol. Now would be a good time to discuss them or to jot them down for discussion later.

Coping with Alcohol was written to provide information on alcohol use and alcoholism and to motivate you to discuss your use of and attitudes toward alcohol with your parents, educators, and peers. The goal of the text is not abstinence, nor is it drinking for all. Rather it is to enable you to clarify your values related to alcohol use; to help you make responsible decisions about the use or nonuse of alcohol; and, if you drink, to help you to lower risks related to drinking and to consider when nondrinking is best for you. It is also a book for nondrinkers, to motivate you to understand your decision regarding nonuse and discuss it as well as why others drink. It is hoped that information and discussion will clear away some of the uncertainties surrounding alcohol and enable teen-agers (and adults as well) to cope with alcohol.

Chapter I

Values Clarification

The ambivalence of society toward alcohol and its use is stressed in the Introduction to explain the attitude that often surrounds alcohol in our country. To further explain our society and to emphasize the importance of values clarification, the environment of drug-taking in the U.S. will be discussed.

The U.S. is a drug-taking society. The use of alcohol for a variety of reasons (as a beverage, to quench a thirst, to forget problems) by approximately 70 percent of the adults is only a part of the picture. Many Americans do not feel that they have gotten their money's worth from a physician if they do not have a prescription in their hands. It is also common for persons to indulge in self-medication from the myriad over-the-counter drugs available. There are drugs to help a person lose weight, stay awake, go to sleep, eliminate body water, alleviate a headache, backache, and other aches, and modify moods. Unfortunately, we as a society are uncomfortable with being uncomfortable. The philosophy seems to be that discomfort is a state that should be eliminated as soon as possible.

Also in our environment is an apparent attitude that happiness and gratification should be immediate. The need for instant gratification as well as instant relief from discomfort are part of society. The buy now–pay later philosophy is only one example of this attitude. Another example is the idea that if one of something is good, two must be better. There is a real danger when the need to be comfortable and happy is combined with the need for instant satisfaction. This change is obvious when a person takes a substance to modify a mood and then takes more of the same substance or another substance to feel the desired effect sooner.

Because of the ambivalence and attitudes surrounding alcohol and other mood-modifying substances, teen-agers receive many messages. Most of these messages are indirect. For example, if you have seen an adult get behind the wheel of a car when intoxicated, the message is probably that it's OK for some people. If you have heard an intoxicated spouse berate and embarrass her husband, you might think that this is acceptable behavior. After all, she's intoxicated. It is not acceptable behavior and should not be excused as such because of intoxication, nor should driving in this state be considered OK. Some of you have already formed many habits and patterns related to alcohol use. The examples above highlight problem areas. It is also true that some of you have very positive and healthy attitudes. If you have witnessed your father giving your mother the keys to drive home because he's been drinking, you have probably decided that it's *not* OK to drink and drive. Though this attitude is a low-risk, healthy one, there is a similarity between both groups. That is, these learnings have not been combined with direct information on what the substance is, why it is being used, how one feels after use, or feelings about problems that could arise. Teen-agers are often in a quandary related to alcohol and their value system.

A person's value system is based on beliefs, opinions,

and attitudes that influence the decisions he/she makes and the actions that he/she takes. However, many adolescents are not aware of what they believe, where those beliefs came from, and on what they will take action. Values clarification means that a person understands why he is doing something and knows that he wants to do it. The theory of values clarification was originally developed by Louis Raths in the 1950's, focusing on helping students be aware of their beliefs, formulate and test judgments, consider alternatives, and make choices. The seven processes of values clarification are:[1]

Prizing one's beliefs and behaviors:
    1. prizing and cherishing
    2. publicly affirming when appropriate
Choosing one's beliefs and behaviors:
    3. from alternatives
    4. after considering consequences
    5. choosing freely
Acting on beliefs:
    6. acting
    7. with pattern, consistency, and repetition.

A nutshell summary of the process is provided in *Health Education: The Search for Values:*

"Values clarification is one approach to improving the quality of life that involves people developing cognitive, affective, active, and interpersonal skills:

---

[1] Raths, L.D., Harmin, M., and Simon, S.B. *Values and Teaching: Working with Values in the Classroom.* Columbus, Ohio: Merrill, 1966.

seeks to help people: 1) clarify their values; 2) feel more valuable; and 3) appreciate the lovability and capability of self and others."[2]

For most of you, your drinking of alcohol has been determined by your family and their drinking patterns. The decision even to drink alcohol may not have been yours. Young children who are given sips of a parent's drink have not made a decision to drink alcohol. As a child grows older, the decision regarding alcohol is often still the family's. Values clarification should cause you to think about your use of alcohol and understand it.

Values clarification is also helpful to a young person who has not even tasted alcohol. You should understand that this nonuse of alcohol has depended on your family's nonuse of alcohol or their feelings about drinking. The family's feeling about nonuse of alcohol (abstinence) can stem from the position of their church, from their parents' feelings, or from problems that they have seen or experienced.

The exercises that follow are values-clarification techniques that can be done alone or with a group. There are no right or wrong answers; any value that you think about, understand, and internalize is acceptable. If you are doing these alone, honesty is the only rule; if a group is using these exercises, acceptance of the ideas of others and respect are added. No put-downs, verbal or in body language, are allowed.

Hopefully, the values-clarification techniques will help you:

[2] Goodman, J., Reed, D., and Simon, S. *Health Education: The Search for Values*. New York: Prentice-Hall, 1977.

1. to clarify your feelings about alcohol and alcoholism;
2. to critically examine facts about alcohol and alcoholism;
3. to understand alcohol use as it is related to the alcohol use of your parents, religious beliefs, ethnic customs;
4. to understand the reasons why people use or do not use alcohol;
5. to clarify the position alcohol plays in your life;
6. to develop the habit of having your values influence day-to-day decisions regarding the use or nonuse of alcohol;
7. to put in perspective the right to abstain, all of the time or some of the time, with the issue of peer pressure;
8. to motivate you to discuss alcohol and its use or nonuse with your parents as well as your peers; and
9. to enable you to seek alternative highs.

VALUES CLARIFICATION EXERCISES

Word Association

Think about what the word "drinker" means to you. Jot down all of the words that come to mind associated with the meaning of "drinker."

Look over your list and share it if others are present.

Now look at your list again. Identify all words that are positive with a check ($\sqrt{}$). Put a circle ($\bigcirc$) next to words that are negative.

Ask yourself or discuss with others the following questions.

How did I define drinking? by number of drinks? by number of drinking occasions? by problems related to alcohol use?

Do I have more positive or more negative feelings about alcohol?

How can I have both positive and negative feelings about the same thing?

Were my feelings due to my thinking about a particular person's alcohol use or my own?

Did I think about alcoholism and not the word "drinker"?

Can the word "drinker" be only positive or only negative when it is related to beverage alcohol?

Enjoyable Activities or Situations

This values-clarification exercise, derived from the rank ordering process, is designed to enable you to understand

and clarify information regarding various alternatives, provide a clarifying personal view of the decision-making process, and enable you to put your alcohol use in perspective. List on a sheet of paper the activities that you enjoy (such as boating, partying, reading). Read over your list and rank the items in order of preference. Then circle those activities on the list during which alcohol would be consumed by you.

Look over your list and ask yourself the following questions:

Are most of the activities I enjoy alcohol-related? or not?

If I tend to prefer activities where I can drink, do I know why?

Is it because I am uncomfortable with other people? Do I feel it's not a good time if alcohol is not served?

If none of the activities are alcohol-related, am I uncomfortable when others are drinking? Is this because of their actions or because of my feelings about alcohol?

Completing the Thought

The following incomplete sentences are designed to help you to clarify your beliefs, to identify areas in which you lack information, and to motivate you to learn more about alcohol and alcoholism.

The best cure for a hangover is _____

Alcohol is a drug that _____

Drinkers are people who _____

Alcoholism is a _____

The effects of alcohol are related to _____

A student who drinks in school should be _____

It would be better for society if alcohol were _____

When young children drink with their parents they are being _____

A blackout is _____

Beer, wine, and distilled spirits all contain _____

People consume alcohol because _____

Alcoholics are people who _____

The ones who suffer from the disease of alcoholism are _____

Alcohol use is part of _____

Synergism is dangerous because _____

Role-playing

Role-playing is an enjoyable as well as a valuable experience. It requires more than one person, though, for the characters and also for discussion. The following are a few suggestions for role-playing situations.

A friend trying to persuade his or her buddy to drink.

A small group of friends at a party trying to get Herb, who is already drunk, to stop drinking.

An intoxicated person arguing with friends that he or she is all right to drive.

A teen-ager trying to convince her mother that the mother is an alcoholic and needs help.

An older brother explaining their mother's alcoholism to a younger brother or sister.

A girl explaining to her intoxicated date why she will not let him drive her home.

A teen-ager explaining to her nonalcoholic parent why she goes to Alateen.

When your group has tried a few of these role-playing situations, design some of your own.

After each role-playing situation each player should explain how he/she felt in the role and what motivated their actions in the situation. The group as well as the role-players should react to the parts played and suggest other outcomes to the situation. Other observations may be encouraged and may even set the stage for a role-playing situation in which a role is acted from a different perspective.

Discussion Questions

Open discussion of relevant questions or topics is also a values-clarification technique. To discuss an issue you must first decide on your position and be able to explain your reasons. In questioning the views of others, you will reinforce or redefine your position. If you are reading the questions alone, think about how you would answer.

Why do most adults drink?

Why do you think most teen-agers drink?

What would you do if one of your parents were an alcoholic?

Do you know an alcoholic?

How do you know that person is an alcoholic?

How do you think most adults feel about teen-age drinking?

How do you think people feel about alcoholics?

What would you do if the person who was to drive you home were drunk?

Suppose that person were your father, would you handle the situation differently than if the driver were a friend?

How would you feel if your date were high? What would you do?

Have you discussed with your parents alternatives for getting the car home if you're drunk?

Do you think there should be a minimum age for the purchase of alcoholic beverages?

What would you do if you thought your friend had a drinking problem?

What would you do if a good friend of yours told you he thought you had a drinking problem?

Which is least harmful—to drink or to smoke?

What do you think would be the most effective way to discourage heavy drinking?

Who do you think would be the best person to tell you facts about alcohol and drugs (for instance, policeman, clergyman, doctor, teacher, ex-addict)?

Do you think there is an alcohol problem with teenagers in your school?

What would you do if you were at a party and didn't want the drink your friends were urging on you?

Have you ever thought about why some people don't drink?

Do you think the U.S. should try Prohibition again? Why?

Is it easy to purchase alcohol and drugs in your community?

Do you think this is because adults don't know or don't care?

What do you think are the signs of a problem drinker?

What is alcoholism?

How do individuals in the U.S. relieve pain?

How many ways of getting "high" can you think of?

Are they high-risk highs or low-risk highs?
If your boyfriend or girlfriend were depressed, how
would you help?

Values Continuum

This values-clarification technique is designed to enable
you to define your values. Following each question or
statement, a range is provided. You may choose to place
yourself on either side or somewhere in the middle. If
your position is in between, attempt to describe your
value.

How far will you go for your group's approval?

Do anything at all.　　　　　　———————　　　　　　Do nothing.

Do you think your parents should set rules for use or
nonuse of alcohol?

Clear rules.　　　　　　———————　　　　　　No rules.

Alcohol use is an important part of our society.

Alcoholism is a major　　———————　Alcohol is a benefit to all of
health problem for our　　　　　　　　　　　　society.
society; therefore alcohol is
a detriment to society.

It is important that laws regulate the age of purchase of
alcoholic beverages.

Laws are important as age　———————　There should be no laws
of purchase must be　　　　　　　　　　restricting purchase of
restricted.　　　　　　　　　　　　　　　alcohol.

In our society nondrinkers should not feel uncomfortable.

Nondrinkers should be uncomfortable because they make drinkers uneasy.	_____	Everyone has a right to be a nondrinker.

Clarifying Statements

The following sentence beginnings are presented to enable you to think about alcohol and its use in your life.

I learned that _____

I realize that _____

I would like to learn more about _____

I would like to discuss _____

I would like to ask my parents _____

I would like to hear what my friends have to say about _____

Interview

Although many adolescents have questions about alcohol use in their lives, it is often not easy to discuss these questions with parents. Yet parents and concerned adults often wish to discuss alcohol and other topics with their teen-agers and have trouble doing so.

A few starter questions are presented to enable you to

interview your parents or other adults. Feel free to add your own or to first use a few to get the discussion started.

FOR DRINKERS:	FOR NONDRINKERS:
How do you feel about drinking?	How do you feel about drinking?
Why do you drink?	Why do you drink?
Have our family always been drinkers?	Have our family always been nondrinkers?
How old were you when you began drinking?	How old were you when you decided to be a nondrinker?
Who influenced this decision?	Who influenced this decision?
Are your reasons for drinking today the same as they were?	Are your reasons for not drinking today the same as they were?
How do you feel about my use or nonuse of alcohol?	How do you feel about my use or nonuse of alochol?
What is appropriate for me?	What is appropriate for me?
How much is too much?	How much is too much?
How do I handle friends wanting me to drink more than I want?	How do I handle friends wanting me to drink?
What are my alternatives for getting home if I happen to have had too much?	What are my alternatives for getting home if I or my friend the driver happens to have had too much?

Search for Alternatives

A few brief story plots are presented for your use. After reading each, list as many alternatives as possible that would be available to the main character. Decide which alternative you would be most comfortable with if you were the main character.

Susie has been dying to go out with Joe for months. She has even taken algebra and physics courses to get to know him. He finally asked her to go to Friday's party at the beach. Susie has been floating on air all week. Friday night's date and party were going great until Joe began drinking and drinking and drinking. The party has ended, and Susie ...

Nick is the eldest and only male in his family. His parents and three sisters are proud of his accomplishments in school and on the basketball team. Nick feels great pressure to live up to everyone's expectations for him and at the same time wants to be a part of his group. After every basketball game the gang goes to a friend's house to celebrate. Nick has always made excuses not to go or to leave early, as he does not like to drink. However, tonight he ...

Everyone in the gang has taken a turn to have the group over for a party. Jane has gone to all the parties and knows that her turn is coming up next. Jane's parents do not approve of under-age persons drinking, and Jane knows that they would not let anyone in with alcohol or would put a friend out if alcohol was sneaked into the house. Jane is feeling caught between her parents' standards and the type of party expected by her friends. As the group begins to discuss where to gather on Friday night, Jane ...

Paper Bag

Each of us wears an invisible paper bag. We put on that bag things we want people to know or things we want people to think about us. Inside the bag are secrets about us that we don't want to share.

Take a minute and write down the things you share on your paper bag; these could also include the way you want people to think about you (lovable, happy, secure). Now think about what you would put on the inside. Perhaps you would write that you're afraid of not being liked or that you think you're a phony. Think about how what you have hidden compares with what you show to others. Think about trying to share one of your secrets with a friend, or if you don't like that part of yourself, how you could change it.

Collage

Advertisements of alcoholic beverages make a great collage, as do drinking scenes found in pictures or stories. Assemble a collection of pictures and describe what feelings each evokes in you. By then assembling them in a collage format, analyze your feelings and attitudes related to drinking in our society. If someone else has a collection or collage, see if the same feelings and attitudes are aroused by a different grouping.

Alcohol Scrabble

Alcohol scrabble is played the same way as Scrabble, but with only alcohol-related words. For example:

```
F E R M E N T A T I O N
        L
        C
        O
        H
        O
        L I Q U O R
                Y
                E
```

What Would You Do If:

- One of your parents had a drinking problem?
- You often smelled alcohol on the breath of a favorite teacher?
- One of your friends was always getting "high"?
- You were concerned about your drinking?
- You were at a party and the group was trying to persuade a nondrinker to drink?
- You were afraid to get together with friends if you hadn't had one or two drinks?
- Your best friend wanted to drive and he/she was intoxicated?
- You always drank to get intoxicated?
- Your friend told you that he/she could not invite you home because of an alcoholic parent?
- You thought someone you loved was an alcoholic?

The values-clarification techniques presented hopefully made you think about your feelings and attitudes related to alcohol use. Although understanding your values is an important goal of the text, an equally important objective is to provide honest, objective, and relevant information. The sections that follow present information in question-and-answer form on alcohol, attitudes toward and use of alcohol, the effects of alcohol on the human body, alcohol problems, and alcoholism. After you have read the sections, look over the values-clarification exercises again and be sure to think about the questions in the discussion section.

Chapter II

Alcohol: Nature and History

1. What are the alcohols?

Alcohols are organic compounds; that is, they contain carbon, a substance produced by living or once-living organisms. Alcohols are a combination of carbon, hydrogen, and oxygen. Though there are hundreds of compounds called alcohols, there are five main types of alcohol: amyl, butyl, ethyl, methyl, and propyl.

2. How are the five most common alcohols used?

Amyl alcohol is a colorless and sharp-smelling alcohol that is mainly derived from fusel oil or can be manufactured synthetically for use as a solvent.

Butyl alcohol is sometimes called butanol. It is used extensively in insect sprays and special types of paint (such as asphalt paint) and is also used as a solvent.

Ethyl alcohol, often called ethanol, is the alcohol in various types of alcoholic beverages (beer, wine, whisky). That is, ethyl alcohol is part of these beverages; no beverage is 100 percent alcohol. Denatured ethyl alcohol (mixed with a poison such as formaldehyde that makes it unfit for human consumption) is used as a solvent and in paints, dyes, and varnishes.

Methyl alcohol, sometimes called wood alcohol, is used as an industrial solvent for dyes, in antifreeze, and in spirit varnishes and paint removers. Methyl alcohol is also mixed with ethyl alcohol to produce rubbing alcohol, a poison when taken internally.

Propyl alcohol, called propanol, is derived mainly from petroleum gases, though it can also be manufactured synthetically. Propyl alcohol is primarily used as a solvent, though it is also used in rubbing alcohol and as a lacquer thinner.

3. Which alcohol do people drink? What happens if you drink other alcohols?

Ethyl alcohol is the only alcohol that is safe for humans to drink, because it is more easily changed into substances that can be eliminated by the body and does not accumulate in the body. Other alcohols are not converted into harmless materials after consumption; rather they are changed into poisons that can accumulate in the body. For example, the consumption of methyl alcohol can produce blindness or death.

4. What is ethyl alcohol?

Ethyl alcohol is a colorless and odorless liquid that is able to mix with water. It is an ingredient in any alcoholic beverage (wine, beer, distilled beverages).

The chemical formula for ethyl alcohol is CH_3CH_2OH, which can also be written C_2H_5OH.

Note: Ethyl alcohol will be called only alcohol in the remaining questions.

5. Is alcohol a food?

Alcohol is classified as a food; it is oxidized (united with oxygen) by the body to produce energy and form carbon dioxide and water. Oxidation of alcohol provides the body with calories as does food; 1 oz. of alcohol produces about 163 calories. However, alcohol does not provide the body with the nutrients found in food.

6. Is alcohol a drug?

Most people think of the term "drug" as meaning prescription medication or the illegal drugs such as heroin, cocaine, or LSD. Since alcohol is not a prescription medication or one of the illegal drugs, most people are not aware that it is a drug. Though alcohol is a socially accepted, legal substance, it is a drug that acts as a depressant on the central nervous system.

7. Is alcohol a stimulant or a depressant (upper or downer)?

Alcohol is incorrectly thought of as a stimulant (a drug that speeds up the activity of the central nervous system). Alcohol is actually a depressant (a drug that slows the activity of the central nervous system).

When a person has a small amount of alcohol (one or two cocktails, glasses of wine, or glasses of beer) he/she is apt to feel more lively and stimulated. This feeling is real

Chemical formula for ethyl alcohol

$$H-\overset{\displaystyle \overset{H}{|}}{\underset{\displaystyle \underset{H}{|}}{C}}-\overset{\displaystyle \overset{H}{|}}{\underset{\displaystyle \underset{H}{|}}{C}}-OH^*$$

* The chemical representation is given for one molecule of the compound. H represents hydrogen; C represents carbon; and OH stands for a union of oxygen and hydrogen, often called a hydroxy.

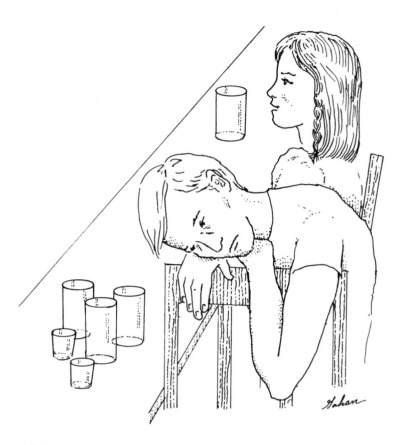

Is Alcohol a Stimulant or a Depressant?

enough, but it is due to the relaxing effects of alcohol and its effects on the person's feelings rather than on his/her central nervous system. The fact that alcohol is a depressant on the central nervous system is obvious when one considers a person who has had quite a bit to drink in a relatively short period of time (4 or 5 cocktails or glasses of wine or beer). As the central nervous system is slowed and dulled, speech becomes slurred, reaction time is impaired, and walking is more of a stagger. Unfortunately, the drinker often does not hear the slurred speech or realize the difficulty in walking. Rather, the drinker still feels buoyed by the alcohol. If drinking continues, the person will pass out and the depressant effects of alcohol will be obvious. If a person could consume more alcohol and reach and reach a Blood Alcohol Concentration of 0.5 percent, a deep coma and danger of death would ensue.

8. If alcohol is a drug, why is it legal?

As mentioned, most people don't think of alcohol as a drug, though it is a depressant on the central nervous system with short-term nonaddictive effects for most of those who consume it. That is, even if a person drank enough beverage alcohol to pass out and had a terrible hangover the next day, by evening he/she would not normally crave another drink, though another drink might be consumed because he/she wanted to have one. However, if the person were a serious problem drinker or an alcoholic, the body might need a drink to function. The disease process related to alcohol usually takes at least five to seven years to develop. This is not the case with substances such as heroin or LSD. When these substances are taken continually or regularly, the addictive process begins. Also in the case of "hard drugs" such as heroin, one needs take an increasingly larger amount to get the same results. In a relatively few short weeks, more of the drug is needed to get a "high" or feeling of euphoria.

Although alcohol differs from other drugs, some people do not feel that it should be legal. This position is understandable when one considers that there are approximately 6 million alcoholics in the U.S. today and perhaps another 4 million problem drinkers; each person with an alcohol problem directly affects the life of at least three other people. On the other hand, the majority of the people who use alcohol do so appropriately and responsibly, not causing problems to themselves or others, and should not be deprived of their right to purchase and consume beverage alcohol. Prohibition (forbidding of the sale, manufacture, and transportation of beverage alcohol) was unsuccessfully tried in the U.S. between 1919 and 1933. It would be foolish to think that another attempt to eliminate alcohol would eliminate alcohol problems.

9. Who discovered alcohol?

No one person or group is given credit for the discovery of alcohol. It was probably discovered by accident when the juice of fruits, berries, or vegetables was left out in the air. After a time, the process of fermentation (see question 17) occurred, and the juice became wine. As an unsuspecting primitive man drank this beverage, the discovery occurred. Since the taste and effects of the wine were found to be pleasurable, primitive man began to duplicate this natural phenomenon and produce his own wine.

10. When was alcohol discovered?

No one knows when alcohol was discovered, just as there is no record of the discovery or discoverers of alcohol. However, we do know that beverage alcohol was used by primitive peoples and recorded as early as 10,000 years ago in the Neolithic period and by early European civilizations.

Making Beer from Chonta Palm Fruit in Ecuador

11. Is alcohol important to society?

Alcohol has been and is a significant part of society. Alcohol use among primitive people, early and medieval civilizations, and European cultures has been recorded. Alcoholic beverages also played an important role in the colonization of our country. When the Puritans set sail for the New World they carried 42 tons of beer and 14 tons of water. Manufacture of alcoholic beverages began in the colonies, and the beverages were then exported to England. After the Revolutionary War the government of the U.S. grew in power and began taxing the alcoholic beverages produced by farmers. The "Whisky Rebellion" followed and was fought by those farmers who did not want to pay the high taxes. Other farmers did not fight but moved to territories not yet states. As years passed, beverage alcohol was still produced and taxed. People opposed to the use of alcoholic beverages formed groups (for instance, the Woman's Christian Temperance Union) to rally for Prohibition. The Eighteenth Amendment to the Constitution, passed in 1919 and declared law in 1920, prohibited the manufacture, sale, or transportation of alcoholic beverages; 177,000 saloons, 1,247 breweries and 507 distilleries were closed in 1920. The law's unpopularity and unenforceability caused its repeal 13 years later. However, this period of time left the country with very vague and unsure feelings about whether alcohol use was good or bad.

Though no major controversies surrounding alcohol use are apparent today, ambivalent feelings about alcohol and its use still exist. Alcohol use is a part of life in the U.S. today and affects all people, drinkers and non-drinkers.

RUTGERS UNIVERSITY CENTER OF ALCOHOL STUDIES
HISTORICAL PICTURE COLLECTION

Temperance

12. What was the Temperance Movement?

The Temperance Movement began in the 1800's in the U.S. Originally it stressed moderate use of beverage alcohol; its emphasis then changed to abstinence from distilled spirits and encouragement to drink beer; and finally it progressed to abstinence from all beverages containing alcohol. Many organizations such as the Anti-Saloon League and the Woman's Christian Temperance Union supported the goals of the movement and actively campaigned for Prohibition.

13. What was Prohibition?

Prohibition in the U.S. was passed in 1919 by the Eighteenth Amendment to the Constitution and became law in 1920. It prohibited the manufacture, sale, and transportation of alcoholic beverages; however, it did not make the purchase or use of alcoholic beverages illegal. The Volstead Act, also passed in 1919, gave Congress and the states the power of enforcement. Enforcement was difficult, as the demand for alcohol still existed and availability of alcohol was assured by private enterprise. In fact, an alcohol-use subculture developed through "bootleggers," "rum-runners," and "speakeasies."

14. What Amendment repealed Prohibition?

As it became apparent that Prohibition was undermining law enforcement and demoralizing public belief in the federal judicial system, the Twenty-first Amendment to the Constitution was passed in 1933. This Amendment, popularly called Repeal, ended Prohibition and again permitted alcoholic beverages to be made and sold to the American public.

Chapter III

Alcoholic Beverages

15. What are alcoholic beverages?

Any beverage that contains alcohol is an alcoholic beverage (beer, wine, and distilled spirits).

16. What are the most popular alcoholic beverages?

Beer is the most widely consumed alcoholic beverage, followed by distilled spirits and wine in the U.S.

17. How is alcohol made?

Alcohol is produced by a natural chemical reaction called fermentation. When the juice of fruits, berries, or vegetables is left unsealed, yeast (a microscopic plant that floats freely in the air) reacts with the sugar in the juice. This reaction produces alcohol in the juice and releases carbon dioxide to the air. Fermentation continues until there is about 12 to 14 percent alcohol in the juice, which is now called wine. At this point there is enough alcohol present to stop the action of the yeast, and the process of fermentation ceases. This process can be illustrated as follows:

Glucose + Yeast $\longrightarrow$ Ethyl Alcohol + Carbon Dioxide
   (Sugar)   yields

The process of fermentation is also used commercially to produce alcohol.

18. How does the natural process of fermentation differ from the commercial one?

For fermentation to occur naturally, the juice of fruits, berries, or grapes need only be exposed to the air. When the process of fermentation is used commercially to produce alcohol, yeast is usually added to the juice of fruits, berries, or vegetables, and this mixture is sealed in a container.

19. Can liquids other than the juice of fruits, berries, or vegetables be fermented?

Yes, any liquid containing glucose (sugar) can be fermented. For example, dandelion wine is the fermented juice of dandelions; birch wine is the fermented juice of tree sap; and honey wine (mead) is the fermented juice of honey.

However, most wines are produced by the fermentation of the juice of grapes.

20. What alcoholic beverages are made by fermentation?

Wine and beer are the two types of beverage alcohol produced by the process of fermentation.

21. What is wine?

Wine is a fermented beverage that can contain from 8 to 14 percent alcohol as a result of natural fermentation; however, many wines contain 12 to 14 percent alcohol by volume. Although most wine is made from grapes, it can also be produced from other fruits or vegetables. Wines

Wine-Making Press

are of various kinds. By color there are white wine, red wine, and rosé (a pink wine). The color depends on the type of grape used. White wines are made from white or skinless black grapes and are actually pale yellow in color; red wines are made from dark grapes. Wines also differ by taste—sweet or dry wines. A sweet wine contains a significant amount of unfermented sugar; a dry wine contains only a small amount of unfermented sugar. A "sparkling" wine results when a substantial amount of carbon dioxide remains in the mixture after fermentation; champagne is an example of a sparkling wine. Sparkling wines can also be made by pumping carbon dioxide into the wine after the process of fermentation has ceased.

22. What is table wine?

Table wine is a fermented beverage that contains approximately 12 to 14 percent alcohol and is normally consumed as a beverage with a meal.

23. What is a fortified wine?

The natural process of fermentation stops when there is approximately 8 to 14 percent alcohol in the wine. When additional alcohol is added to wine to bring the alcohol content to approximately 20 percent the wine is called fortified. Port and sherry are examples of fortified wines.

24. What is the difference between a table wine, a dessert wine, and a fortified wine?

A table wine is a wine that is usually consumed with meals such as white wine or rosé; it is produced naturally or commercially and is unfortified.

A dessert wine is a sweet wine such as tokay or marsala that is usually served after dinner; it contains a residue of unfermented sugar.

Fortified wines such as sherry, port, and madeira are wines to which additional alcohol was added during or after fermentation. The alcohol content of fortified wines is about 20 percent.

25. What is beer?

Beer is an alcoholic beverage made by the fermentation of cereal grains such as corn, rye, wheat, or barley; beer contains between 3 percent and 6 percent alcohol.

26. How is beer made?

Beer is produced by a process called brewing. A liquid mixture of yeast and a malted cereal such as corn, rye, wheat, or barley is fermented to produce alcohol and carbon dioxide. Fermentation is stopped before the yeast completes its action to limit the beverage's alcohol content to between 3 percent and 6 percent. Tiny dried buds of the hop vine, called hops, are added to the beer for flavor. The addition of hops also helps to preserve the beer.

27. What is ale?

Ale is a fermented beverage made from the same ingredients as beer. However, the ale-making process (top fermentation) differs from that of beer (lager type,

MUSEUM OF THE CITY OF NEW YORK

Brewery, New York City 1852

bottom fermentation). The alcohol content of ale may be slightly higher than that of beer.

28. What are 3.2 beer, light beer, and low-alcohol beer?

Three point two beer is beer that contains not more than 3.2 percent alcohol. Some states permit sale of 3.2 beer where stronger alcoholic beverages are prohibited. The age at which one is allowed to purchase 3.2 beer often differs from that at which one may buy other alcoholic beverages. Light beer is one reduced in calorie content; low-alcohol beer has lower alcohol content. Both are contemporary additions to the alcohol beverage market.

29. What is near-beer?

Near-beer is a fermented beverage made from the same ingredients and in the same process as beer. The

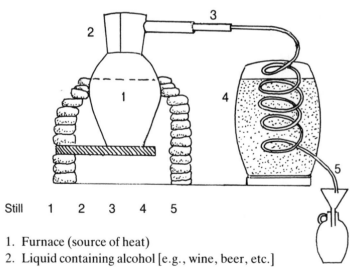

Still   1   2   3   4   5

1. Furnace (source of heat)
2. Liquid containing alcohol [e.g., wine, beer, etc.]
3. Vapor
4. Condenser (steam cooled to liquid)
5. Product containing higher percent of alcohol

alcohol is then removed so that near-beer contains only about ½ percent alcohol.

30. What is distillation?

Distillation is the process of converting a liquid into a vapor by means of heat; the vapor is then condensed into a liquid state by cooling. The purpose of distillation is to separate one liquid from another liquid or to separate a liquid from solids.

31. How are other types of alcoholic beverages produced?

Alcoholic beverages are also produced by the process of distillation. A fermented beverage (wine or beer) is heated in a device called a still. Since alcohol vaporizes (becomes a gas) at 78°C and water vaporizes at 100°C, the alcohol separates from the mixture and becomes particles of moisture. The water and the other ingredients of the wine or beer remain in the liquid state. The alcohol vapor is then captured and cooled. As the vapor cools, it returns to liquid form and is almost pure alcohol. Flavoring and additional water are then added to produce the alcoholic beverage with the desired amount of alcohol. The process of distillation is used to produce alcoholic beverages that contain at least 25 percent alcohol.

32. What beverages are made by distillation?

Whisky, gin, vodka, and rum are examples of alcoholic beverages made by the process of distillation.

33. How are the different types of distilled beverages made?

Distilled beverages are mainly flavored alcohol and water. Distillation of the fermented juice of fruits or grain produces a liquid that contains a high amount of alcohol, flavoring, and some water. Whisky (rye, scotch, bourbon) is made by distilling the fermented juice of cereal grains such as corn, rye, and barley. Gin is a combination of alcohol, water, and flavors. Vodka, distilled from rye malt, fermented potatoes, apples, or other fruits, is mostly a mixture of alcohol and water. Rum is produced from fermented molasses or sugarcane juice.

Distillation of wine produces brandies. Liqueurs are made by adding sugar and flavoring to a brandy or to a combination of alcohol and water.

34. What are degrees of "proof"?

Degrees of "proof" indicate the amount of alcohol contained in distilled beverages. Every bottle of distilled beverages sold in the U.S. has the degrees of "proof" listed on its label. Dividing the proof by two gives the alcohol content; that is, 90-proof scotch contains 45 percent alcohol.

35. What is liquor?

The word liquor is another name for beverage alcohol. However, it is most often used to mean only distilled beverages and not wine or beer.

36. How much alcohol is in wine, beer, and distilled beverages?

Beverages and their corresponding alcohol content are as follows:

Beverage	Alcohol Content
Wine	12 to 14%
Fortified wine	20%
Beer	3 to 6%
Distilled beverages (whisky, scotch, gin, rum, vodka)	40 to 50%

37. What is brandy?

Brandy is a distilled beverage that contains about 40 percent alcohol. It is made by the process of distillation (explained in question 31) from wine. Cognac is a brandy made from grape wine in the Cognac region of France.

The word brandy is also used when fruit wine (made from fruits other than grapes) is distilled. Plum brandy, apple brandy, and cherry brandy are examples of brandies made from other types of fruit wines.

38. What are liqueurs?

Liqueurs are sweet distilled beverages that contain between 20 percent and 65 percent alcohol. Liqueurs are made in three ways:

1. by distilling a mixture of flavors (e.g., fruits or herbs) and a beverage with a high percentage of alcohol;
2. by adding flavors (e.g., fruits or herbs) to a brandy; or

3. by adding sugar, water, and flavoring to alcohol.

Liqueurs are usually consumed after dinner; Benedictine, Drambuie, and Crème de Menthe are examples of liqueurs.

39. What is a cocktail?

A cocktail is a mixture of a distilled beverage (usually 1½ oz.) with other highly flavored ingredients. The flavoring ingredients may be wines, liqueurs, fruits, vegetables, milk, or others. There are over a thousand cocktail recipes, yet only about fifty of these are commonly used. Martini (vermouth, gin or vodka), Tequila Sunrise (tequila, orange juice, grenadine), Manhattan (whisky, sweet vermouth, bitters) are examples of cocktails.

40. What is a highball?

A highball is a mixture of a distilled beverage (usually 1½ oz.) such as whisky or scotch with water or a carbonated beverage such as ginger ale. This drink is usually served in a tall glass with ice.

41. What is the alcohol beverage industry?

The alcohol beverage industry is the industry that manufactures beverage alcohol; it also includes other companies that bottle, transport, and sell alcoholic beverages. Approximately 2 million people are employed in the various segments of the alcohol beverage industry.

42. Does the alcohol beverage industry pay taxes?

Every alcoholic beverage that is produced for sale is taxed by the federal government. In fact, the amount collected in taxes from the sale of beverage alcohol is second only to corporate and personal taxes as a source of revenue for the U.S. government. Each state also imposes taxes on all beverage alcohol that is sold.

43. Does the alcohol beverage industry contribute to society?

The alcohol beverage industry makes two obvious contributions to society:

1. the employment of approximately 2 million people in the manufacture, transportation, and sale of alcoholic beverages; and
2. the second-largest source of tax revenue for the U.S. government.

There is also a less obvious contribution made by the alcohol beverage industry; that is, the availability of alcohol. Since most people use alcohol in appropriate ways and for acceptable reasons, the ability to purchase alcohol meets the needs of a large group of people in society.

There are also societal problems related to alcohol use that must be discussed; alcoholism is the most significant of these problems. Some groups believe that if alcohol were not available (an almost impossible feat, as shown in the information on Prohibition), there would be no alcoholics. Of course, this is true. Yet alcoholics have complex problems that are not generated by the availability of the substance of abuse.

Chapter IV

Attitudes Toward Alcohol

44. Do people feel differently about alcohol use and nonuse?

Yes, most definitely, individuals and groups feel differently regarding the use or nonuse of alcohol. The most obvious example of this was Prohibition and Repeal. During that time the country was divided into the "wets"—those who thought alcohol was "good" and should be available to all, and the "drys"—those who thought alcohol was "evil" and should be prohibited. Though this vocal argument ceased, the mixed feelings about alcohol remained, and today alcohol use can be characterized as in an ambivalent state. Its use is legal and considered socially acceptable, but there is no national pattern of use or consensus regarding use. A person's attitude toward alcohol depends on cultural background, religious affiliation, socioeconomic status, and other factors.

Unfortunately, there are often negative feelings and a lack of understanding on both sides (those who drink and those who do not drink) regarding alcohol use; that is, abstainers do not understand why people drink, and drinkers are often suspicious of nondrinkers.

45. Why do people feel differently about alcohol?

The way a person feels about alcohol depends on many

factors. The first is his family background. Though young people often hate to admit that they have been or are strongly influenced by their parents, this is actually the case. When drinking habits, customs, and beverages are considered, individuals most often mirror the parental drinking practices. In essence, drinking and nondrinking are learned behaviors.

Other factors that influence a person's feelings about alcohol use are religious beliefs, socioeconomic status, and peer group. These factors all affect a person's alcohol use or nonuse in some way.

46. How do you feel about drinking?

The way you feel about drinking stems from many things: your parents' feelings about alcohol, your cultural background, your religion, life experiences related to alcohol, your friends, society. The most amazing thing is that most people rarely think about or analyze their feelings about alcohol. Yet, knowing how you feel about alcohol is extremely important because your feelings will be reflected in your alcohol use. If you are unsure of where you stand, you may be talked into another drink or feel that you have to drink when you don't feel like it.

47. Are there techniques to help you know how you feel about alcohol?

Values-clarification techniques can help a person discover how he feels about many things (e.g., decision-making, truth, sex). These techniques are especially helpful to a person willing to determine his feelings and perspective on alcohol. An easy example of a values-clarification exercise that can be done on a sheet of paper is as follows: List about 20 of the things you like best to do (for example, jogging, partying). Rank the activities in order of preference and then circle those in which alcohol would be consumed. As you look at the circled items, you should be able to get some idea of how important alcohol is in your life.

48. What do people associate with the word "drink"?

The word "drink" produces a negative reaction in many people, as does the word "drinker." These words imply much more than having a drink with dinner; they evoke thoughts of alcohol problems. This is especially true when one discusses the alcohol use of the young. A parent is reluctant to label his child a drinker or answer that his child has had a drink; yet that same parent can affirmatively answer the question "Does your child have a glass of wine at dinner?" with ease.

Chapter V

Adult Alcohol Use and Teen-age Drinking

49. What types of people are drinkers, nondrinkers?

All types of people are drinkers and all types of people are nondrinkers.

50. How many Americans drink?

Approximately half the population of the U.S. (about 100 million) consume alcoholic beverages at some time during a year.

51. Do as many females as males drink?

For many years, more males than females drank, and this is still true when one considers only the adult population. However, recent studies of teen-age drinking indicate that approximately the same percent of females as males (about 70 percent) consume alcoholic beverages, although males usually consume larger quantities.

52. Does a drinker always have to drink when beverage alcohol is served?

No, there are many times in a person's life when alcohol should not be consumed even by someone who considers himself a drinker. If you are tired, upset, or depressed, alcohol may make you more tired, more upset, or more depressed.

It is sad that, in our society, one who chooses not to drink on an occasion may be considered unsociable; people need to clarify their feelings about alcohol and its place in their lives. By understanding this, the right to not-drink will also be understood.

53. How many people in the U.S. do not drink?

Approximately 30 percent of the adult population does not drink beverage alcohol. That is, 3 out of 10 Americans do not consume alcoholic beverages; these people are called abstainers.

54. Why do some people not drink?

Most people who choose not to drink alcoholic beverages do so because of religious convictions. However, there are other reasons for abstaining, among them a dislike of the taste of alcoholic beverages, a dislike of the effects of alcoholic beverages, family background, prior problems with alcohol use, and recovering from alcoholism.

Reasons for not drinking are as legitimate as the majority of the reasons listed for drinking; unfortunately, society does not always accept this. Pressure is often placed on a nondrinker to be "sociable" and have a drink. This implies that one cannot be sociable without drinking. Also, drinkers are often suspicious of their nondrinking companions, probably because they fear judgment of their actions. Nondrinkers themselves are also often uncomfortable in drinking situations. Each point of view needs to be understood by both drinkers and non-drinkers.

55. What proportion of the population in the U.S. are abstainers, light drinkers, moderate drinkers, and heavy drinkers?

In *Alcohol, Science and Society Revisited*[1] Don Cahalan provides the information summarized in the following chart:

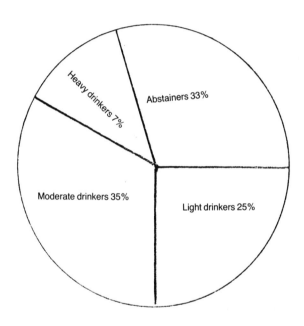

56. What are light drinking, moderate drinking, and heavy drinking?

Light drinking means that a person drinks one to two drinks on occasion. These drinking occasions occur at least once a month and may be more frequent.

[1] Cahalan, D., "Epidemiology: Alcohol Use in American Society" in Gomberg, E., White, H., and Carpenter, J.A., eds, *Alcohol, Science and Society Revisited*, New Brunswick, NJ: Rutgers Center of Alcohol Studies, 1982.

Moderate drinking is consumption of moderate to average amounts of alcohol (three to four drinks on a drinking occasion). The number of drinking occasions is also a factor in defining the term moderate drinking. A moderate drinker could drink two to three times within a week and consume light to moderate amounts of alcohol on each occasion. Extending this definition even further, a moderate drinker could consume one drink a day more often than two to three times a week.

Heavy drinking refers to consumption of large amounts of alcohol (as much as five drinks or more) on a regular and frequent basis.

These definitions are not meant to imply that a person cannot vary from a drinking pattern. There are light and moderate drinkers who occasionally indulge in heavy drinking, as there are heavy drinkers who occasionally drink lightly. However, most drinkers do have a specific alcohol use pattern.

57. What percent of the population of the U.S. drinks alcohol?

Approximately 70 percent of the adult population, or about half of the total population, drinks beverage alcohol. That is, 7 out of 10 adult Americans have a drink of beverage alcohol at some time during a year.

58 Why do people drink?

There are many reasons why people use alcohol. Most of these reasons are based on cultural drinking patterns, family alcohol use patterns, and specifics related to life-style (peers, economic level, social functions). The following are some of the non-problem reasons why most people drink:

- to quench a thirst,
- to be social,
- to relax,
- to use as a mealtime beverage,
- to go to sleep,
- to celebrate an occasion.

A person's reasons for using alcohol depend on his background and how he learned to use alcohol as well as his own feelings and specific circumstances. Most of the people who drink do so responsibly for a variety of acceptable reasons. A person may have a beer after mowing the lawn one day and drink at a party the next day. Yet there are people who do not have a variety of reasons for alcohol use and may only drink when having wine with dinner.

There are also problem reasons why some people drink: to escape, to avoid a problem, to use as a crutch in a difficult situation.

59. Where do people drink?

Most beverage alcohol is consumed in a home situation (as a beverage, at a party, for a celebration). Other places where alcohol is consumed are restaurants, bars, trains, and planes.

60. When do people drink?

When people drink relates directly to why people drink and where they drink. Beverage alcohol that is consumed as a mealtime beverage would be drunk at lunch or dinner. A celebration might be held in the middle of the afternoon, and alcoholic beverages would then be consumed at that time. Dancing in a discotheque might make the time for drinking be quite late at night.

61. What kinds of people drink alcohol?

All kinds of people drink alcohol, and all types of people abstain. There are church-goers, politicians, doctors, lawyers, teachers, and laborers who drink as well as those in these groups who do not.

62. Are there cultural differences related to drinking?

Cultural drinking patterns are distinguishable in our society. The Jews have been noted for the sobriety and control that surrounds their drinking situations. Though drinking is part of religious ceremonies and services (for instance, Kiddush, Rosh Hashanah, and Passover) and also social situations, drunkenness is considered unacceptable.

The Italian tradition of alcohol use has also disapproved of drunkenness. Drinking has centered on mealtime, with wine as the normal beverage.

Different from these patterns was the use of alcohol in old rural Ireland. Drinking was a separate part of life mainly for young men. Heavy use of alcohol in the pubs was accepted, and the drunkard was not condemned. Many of the habits, patterns, and attitudes related to drinking of the Irish in the U.S. today have their roots in the customs of old Ireland.

Though it cannot be said that all Jews or all Italians or all Irish drink in the same manner, it is often true that feelings and attitudes about alcohol use are related to cultural background.

63. Does alcohol have the same effects on men and women?

The effects of alcohol on a person, male or female, depend on a variety of factors. The reason one is drinking and the expectation one has for the results of drinking greatly influence the effects of alcohol. Other things that influence the effects of alcohol are the personality of the drinker, body size, the type of beverage being consumed, the drinking situation, whether she/he is eating while drinking or has recently eaten, and the amount of alcohol consumed. With all these factors related to the effects of alcohol, it is easy to understand how two identical drinks can affect two persons differently, whether male or female. It is also quite possible for a person to be affected differently by the same drinks on different occasions.

64. What is social drinking?

Social drinking once meant the use of beverage alcohol at social functions. It has come to mean the use of beverage alcohol that does not cause problems for the drinkers or others. Drinking before or after dinner, before bed, or after physical work is considered social drinking, as is drinking at a party, celebration, or other type of social function.

65. Do young people make the decision to use or not use beverage alcohol?

The answer to this question is a loud and emphatic NO for most young people. The initial decision to use or not use beverage alcohol is made for children by their parents. When a ten-year-old girl is offered a small glass of champagne to toast her brother's wedding, she has not made a decision to use beverage alcohol. She does not realize that this offer reflects many aspects of her family's background (religion, culture, etc.). The same is true for a young person raised in a nondrinking family. The offer of a drink is not forthcoming, yet this nonuse is also often not clarified.

Added to the fact that family alcohol use or nonuse is not clarified or understood by children is the fact that little attempt is made, by society in general and parents in particular, to help young people understand the other point of view. This failure compounds the ambivalence of feelings regarding alcohol. Drinkers are urged to "hold their liquor" and not be "teetotalers," while nondrinkers discuss drinking as if evil lurked in every bottle. Each position should be understood and respected to enable every person to respect the rights of others.

66. At what age do most young people have their first drink?

Most young people have their first drink between the ages of 11 and 13 at home in family situations. Since the largest proportion of beverage alcohol sold is for home use, this should not be surprising. Many people are uncomfortable when the "drinking" of an 11-year-old is discussed because the word "drinking" implies problem behavior. It is not difficult for a person to accept a child's being given a small glass of wine during a family spaghetti dinner; yet that person has trouble accepting the fact that a 10- or 11-year-old drinks beverage alcohol.

When we realize that most alcohol is consumed in a home situation and for acceptable reasons, it is understandable that young people are invited to partake of alcoholic beverages as they would be invited to join the family in religious services or celebrations.

67. Why do young people start drinking?

Young people learn about drinking from their family. They learn when alcohol is used, why it is used, what type of beverages are consumed, and how much is drunk. Most often it is not the young person who decides if he will use beverage alcohol; rather it is a parental decision. Yet most of us are not aware of the parental influence on the individual's drinking habits. This influence is so direct that most young people from families that abstain from alcohol do not drink; most young people who are from light or moderate drinking families are light or moderate drinkers, and unfortunately many young people who are from heavy drinking families are heavy drinkers. Alcohol use is learned behavior.

Young people are not often helped to understand why their parents use alcohol and therefore do not understand their own personal use. Without this basic understanding, it is often difficult to make decisions related to drinking outside of the family or home setting.

68. How does a teen-ager learn to use beverage alcohol?

A teen-ager learns how to use beverage alcohol from his parents' attitudes toward and use of alcoholic beverages. In most families, he learns when beverage alcohol is used (e.g., mealtime), for what reasons (e.g., beverage), and what type of beverage is consumed (e.g., wine). Another teen-ager may learn quite another type of lesson. He might learn that one drinks (e.g., four or five drinks or more) when a problem arises. Unfortunately, in most parental examples of drinking patterns and behaviors, parents do not attempt to explain their attitudes toward or use of beverage alcohol. Usually this is also the case in nondrinking homes. Values are placed upon children and not clarified. Parental use or nonuse of beverage alcohol is directly related to many factors: religious beliefs, cultural background, economic status, life-style, age, sex. Teen-agers are expected to absorb parental values about alcohol, yet they are taught to challenge other aspects of their life. Teen-agers should be helped to understand their parents' feelings regarding beverage alcohol if they are to be expected to understand their own feelings and patterns of use.

69. Do the drinking habits of children always mirror the drinking habits of their parents?

No, they do not. Most teen-agers experience a period of deviance from many of the parent-held values, patterns, and behaviors. That is, teen-agers often go through a period (a few months in length to a few years) in which they differ from the drinking habits of their parents.

70. What is meant by the "age of deviance" when teen-age drinking is discussed?

The age of deviance refers to a time when young people differ in drinking habits and patterns from those of their parents. Young people are usually introduced to alcohol between the ages of 11 and 13. This initial drinking experience usually takes place with their parents in the home, or it might occur at a family celebration such as a wedding. Most of the alcohol use that continues for a period of time usually follows the drinking habits and patterns of the parents. Teen-agers then begin drinking outside the home and are affected by many experiences and pressures as they mature and seek independence. In their struggle in many life areas, peers are often consulted for guidance and norms of behavior. Alcohol use is affected by these life changes and peer norms (often referred to as peer pressure). The age of deviance related to alcohol use occurs at this time, which may be age 15 to 18. This does not come at the same age for each person, nor under the same conditions. However, it is obvious when one thinks of the drinking patterns in college or military service; drinking in these situations is heavier and more frequent than the pattern of alcohol use for the majority of adults.

Though this period of deviance from parental drinking norms differs in duration for each person, most individuals mature out of frequent heavy drinking by about age 24. By age 24 or thereabouts, most people have set life goals and are independent. As the person reaches this stage, he/she again approximates parental drinking norms in terms of when, why, and how much one drinks. This phenomenon of maturation related to alcohol use must be considered in perspective. Children of light or moderate drinking parents probably will return to light or moderate drinking. However, children of heavy drinking parents or those who consume alcohol problematically may continue in or return to this heavy or problematic pattern.

71. How many teen-agers use alcohol?

Approximately 70 percent of the teen-ager population by age 17–18 drink beverage alcohol. This use of alcoholic beverages may be defined as rare, occasional, or frequent. Included in this percentage are teen-agers who drink only once a year, for religious reasons or during a special family holiday. The greatest proportion of the teen-agers who drink do so appropriately and for acceptable reasons (to relax, to enjoy a social occasion).

Trends in adolescent drinking have recently been identified indicating an "increased prevalence of alcohol use, drinking at earlier ages, increased frequency of intoxication, and a tendency for girls' drinking to more nearly approximate that of boys."[2]

[2] O'Gorman, P.A., et al. *Aspects of Youthful Drinking*, New York: National Council on Alcoholism, 1978.

72. Why do teen-agers drink?

Teen-agers drink for the same reasons that adults give for using beverage alcohol: to quench thirst, to consume as a meal-time beverage, to relax, to be sociable, to enjoy a party. There are also other reasons for alcohol use that are considered inappropriate or problematic.

About 5 percent of the adult drinking population list problem reasons for drinking, as do a small portion of the teen-age drinking population. Examples of problem reasons for alcohol use are to forget worries or problems, to get through a day, to use as a crutch because reality is too difficult, to avoid facing a life situation.

73. How do adults feel about teen-age drinking?

Most adults respond favorably when asked if it is acceptable for teen-agers to have wine at a family dinner, champagne at a sister's wedding, beer after mowing the lawn. The word "drinking," as discussed in question 48, often implies heavy drinking or problem drinking and is frequently not interpreted as consumption of alcohol. Teen-age drinking aside from the type of nonproblem examples listed above is often responded to in a negative fashion by adults.

74. Is it dangerous for teen-agers to drink?

The most serious and immediate threat of alcohol use for teen-agers is intoxication. This is because teen-agers are learning and perfecting a variety of skills, such as social interaction or driving. Since these skills are not fully developed, they require an unimpaired mind. There is also a danger in the fact that newly acquired skills are usually affected first by alcohol.

Adolescent drinking also differs from adult alcohol use

in a variety of ways that should be understood by the teen-ager. Teen-agers, being generally lighter than adults, are affected by alcohol more quickly because one ounce of alcohol will have more effect on a person who weighs 100 lb. than on one who weighs 180 lb. Also, an adolescent's lack of experience with alcohol use may prevent the teen-ager from making correct decisions about his/her drinking.

Regular heavy drinking by a teen-ager could also pose a danger. If drinking is done as an escape or a crutch, it could develop into an alcohol problem. This type of drinking and potential alcohol problem by a teen-ager must be differentiated from an occasional problem that a young person has related to his alcohol use. Most of these occasional problems are not alcohol problems, but rather teen-age adjustment problems. A teen-ager who is asked to leave a school dance on one occasion because of his alcohol use does not have an alcohol problem; he has a social problem related to alcohol. However, a teen-ager who brings a bottle to school to get through the day definitely has an alcohol problem.

A serious danger to teen-agers is the mixing of drugs and alcohol by taking them simultaneously or in sequence. Synergism may result. The synergistic effect is simply explained in that $2 + 2$ does not equal 4. Two drinks plus 2 pills such as barbiturates may equal an effect of 16, producing extreme intoxication, stupor, and even death.

75. How old do you have to be to drink alcohol?

In most states, including New York, New Jersey, and California, parents are allowed to serve alcohol to their children regardless of age in their home or another private place. It is not legal for a parent to buy or serve an alcoholic beverage to an underage child in a public place. In some states a parent is not allowed to serve beverage alcohol to an under-age child even in the home.

Most state laws regarding alcohol have to do with the sale and purchase of beverage alcohol and not its consumption. A movement is currently under way in the U.S. to establish 21 as the national legal age for purchase of beverage alcohol; at this time, however, no single minimum age is in effect throughout the country. Some states have two legal ages: one for the purchase of all types of beverage alcohol except 3.2 beer, and another for 3.2 beer. In New Jersey, for instance, one must be 21 years of age to buy any alcoholic beverage; yet in Colorado a person must be 21 to purchase distilled spirits, beer, and wine but only 18 to purchase 3.2 beer.

76. What is the minimum age law?

The minimum age law refers to the youngest age at which a person may purchase alcoholic beverages. The legal age or minimum age varies from state to state, as does where you can buy alcohol. New Jersey law licenses the selling of beverage alcohol in liquor stores, bars, and restaurants. In Pennsylvania beverage alcohol in bottles can be sold only in state liquor stores, but places such as taverns and restaurants can be licensed to sell beverage alcohol drinks.

77. Why do teen-agers sometimes feel that they have to drink?

Our society has had very vague attitudes about alcohol for a long time. It is considered evil and good at the same time. Society has also encouraged the prevalence of myths related to alcohol. These myths are voiced in clichés, such as "hold one's liquor," "drink like a man," and "drink him under the table." Along with these views, which equate virility and strength with one's ability to drink, is the fact that sociability and the serving of alcohol are often considered one and the same. A host often feels that he must serve a guest a drink of beverage alcohol or he is not being hospitable. In this same situation, a guest is often made to feel that refusal of a drink of beverage alcohol implies that he is not having a good time.

It is no wonder that teen-agers often feel pressure to drink. They have been brought up in this kind of atmosphere and are uncomfortable when they refuse. This is true of young people who drink but on occasion refuse as well as teen-agers who abstain. Unfortunately, adults have not helped the young drinker and nondrinker to clarify their values regarding alcohol use. Nor have these teen-agers been helped to understand the values of the other position. Society's views regarding alcohol will remain vague and ambivalent until values clarification and understanding occur.

78. Does peer pressure influence a teen-ager's drinking?

Peer pressure is usually not the factor that causes a teen-ager to begin drinking. However, it is a significant factor affecting when, where, what, and how much a teen-ager drinks in specific situations.

Though the term peer is usually used when discussing adolescents, it also applies to adults who are members of a group, are of the same age generation, or hold similar status (e.g., professional, socioeconomic). Peer pressure can certainly influence an adult's drinking at a party or business lunch. Many adults are uncomfortable when around others who are not drinking or who are not drinking as much as they are. Pressure is then applied to "relax and have a drink."

79. What percent of the teen-agers who drink have problems related to their use of alcoholic beverages?

The majority of the teen-agers who drink beverage alcohol do so appropriately and responsibly, not causing problems for themselves or others. However, there is a percentage of young people (approximately 5 percent of the teen-age drinking population) who have problems related to alcohol use. Most of these problems when they occur are not alcohol problems per se, but rather behavior problems of which alcohol is an accompanying part: being asked to leave a school dance because of drinking; insulting friends after drinking; getting in trouble with one's parents because of a drinking experience. However, a small group of the teen-agers having problems with alcohol are actually experiencing alcohol problems; that is, their alcohol use causes continual problems for themselves or others. Examples of the problems of this group are drinking in school; often driving after drinking; having fights with parents over drinking; drinking alone; drinking in the morning. These young people need help with their alcohol problem because it usually gets worse, whereas young people who have a once-in-a-lifetime or infrequent problem will probably outgrow it as they learn more about alcohol and themselves.

Chapter **VI**

Effects of Alcohol on the Human Body

80. What are the effects of alcohol on the human body?

The effects of alcohol on the human body and the time it takes alcohol to leave the body are presented in the chart shown on page 60.

81. Does alcohol affect everyone in the same way?

Alcohol affects each person differently depending on the quantity of alcohol consumed, the size of the drinker, the expectations of the drinker, the type of beverage consumed, and the amount of food in the stomach. In fact, alcohol does not always affect the same person in the same manner, because of different mood, expectations, or other factors.

82. Why does alcohol affect people differently?

People differ in size, experience with alcohol, expectations of the effects of alcohol, type of beverage alcohol consumed, amount of alcohol consumed, and time in which alcohol is consumed, and thus are affected by it differently.

Number of Drinks*	Blood Alcohol Concentration	Effects of Alcohol	Time to Leave the Body
1 or 1 or 1	0.03%	Relaxed; slight feeling of exhilaration	2 hours
2 or 2 or 2	0.06%	Slowed reaction time; poor muscle control; slurred speech; legs wobbling	4 hours
3 or 3 or 3	0.09%	Judgment clouded; inhibitions and self-restraint lessened; ability to reason and make logical decisions impaired	6 hours
4 or 4 or 4	0.12%	Vision blurred; unclear speech; stumbles when walking; hands do not work well together	8 hours
5 or 5 or 5	0.15%	All behavior affected; unable to remove clothes; staggers when walking without help; bumps into objects; drops things; activity requiring coordination cannot be performed; difficulty staying awake	10 hours

* Each drink contains 1½ ounces of whisky, gin, or other distilled spirit, or 5 ounces of wine, or 12 ounces of beer.

83. What makes the effects of alcohol on the human
     body different for the same person on different
     occasions?

The effects of alcohol on the body depend on a great
many factors.

The *size of the person* is a factor; the larger the person,
the greater the volume of blood through which alcohol is
dispersed. A teen-ager who is smaller than adult stature
will feel the effects of alcohol more strongly and more
quickly than when the same teen-ager has reached adult
body size and weight.

The size of drink also affects the way the person's body
reacts to alcohol. It is the quantity of alcohol consumed
that determines the speed, type, and duration of its
effects. If a person who usually drinks a 5-oz. glass of
wine drinks a 10-oz. glass, he has actually consumed
twice his normal amount of alcohol and will feel the
effects correspondingly.

The type of beverage alcohol consumed is also a factor
related to the effects of alcohol on the human body.

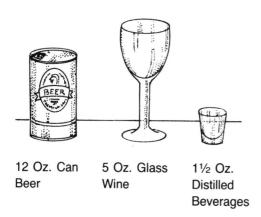

12 Oz. Can	5 Oz. Glass	1½ Oz.
Beer	Wine	Distilled
		Beverages

Various beverages contain different amounts of alcohol. Regular beer contains between 3 and 6 percent alcohol; wine usually contains between 12 and 14 percent alcohol; fortified wine contains 20 percent alcohol; and distilled spirits contain between 40 and 50 percent. However, when these various beverages are served in appropriate glasses, equivalent amounts of alcohol can be found in the beverages illustrated on page 61.

It is obvious that a person who drinks 4½ oz. (3 normal shots) of whisky will consume more alcohol than one who drinks 4½ oz. of wine or beer.

Food in the stomach is also directly related to the effects of alcohol on the human body. Food slows the process by which alcohol is absorbed into the bloodstream. Since the effects of alcohol are not felt by the person until the alcohol is in the bloodstream, food will slow this process and thereby minimize the effects. A person who usually has a drink after dinner will feel the effects of a cocktail before dinner more strongly since his stomach does not contain food.

The *length of time* during which one drinks is also related to the effects of alcohol. This time period is related to the number of drinks. If a person has four drinks of beer, wine, or whisky of equivalent alcohol content in six hours, it is unlikely that he will experience any obvious effects of alcohol. However, if the same person has the same four drinks in a one-hour period, he will most certainly feel the effects of alcohol.

Quantity of beverage alcohol consumed is also a factor in the effects of alcohol. As mentioned, it is the alcohol in the various beverages that produces the effects on the human body. Therefore, the more alcohol consumed, the more likely and obvious will be the effects.

The *feelings and expectations* of the drinker also affect

how he/she reacts to alcohol. If a person is tense and drinks quickly, he will experience the effects of alcohol more strongly than if he were more relaxed. Also, if a person expects alcohol to buoy his spirits or make him more sociable, this is the initial reaction he will obtain from drinking.

All of these factors influence the way a person reacts to alcohol and the subsequent effects he experiences. It should be quite easy to understand how the effects of alcohol on the same person can be quite different on two different occasions.

84. What does "alcohol makes a person feel differently" mean?

One of the effects of alcohol is that it makes a person "feel differently." One drink of alcohol relaxes a person and gives him a slight feeling of exhilaration. Continuing consumption of alcohol may lessen a person's self-restraint and loosen inhibitions; in this condition a person would not only feel differently but also act differently.

85. How does one measure the amount of alcohol present in a person's blood?

Blood Alcohol Concentration is the term used to designate the amount of alcohol in a person's blood. Blood Alcohol Concentration (BAC) is always written as a decimal part of 1 percent. If a person's BAC were between 0.5 percent and 1 percent, the breathing center of the brain would be paralyzed and death would occur. Since alcohol usually causes a person to pass out before being able to consume enough alcohol for a BAC of such a level, this rarely occurs. See also question 98.

There are many types of devices that measure the

percentage of alcohol in the blood by analyzing breath, urine, or blood samples.

86. How does alcohol affect the body?

Alcohol has a physiological (physical) effect on the body; it depresses the central nervous system. A small amount of alcohol (one to two drinks) increases the stomach's secretion of gastric juices and thereby increases the appetite. The intestines become stimulated by the alcohol, and the urine flow from the kidneys is increased.

Larger amounts of alcohol (three to four drinks)

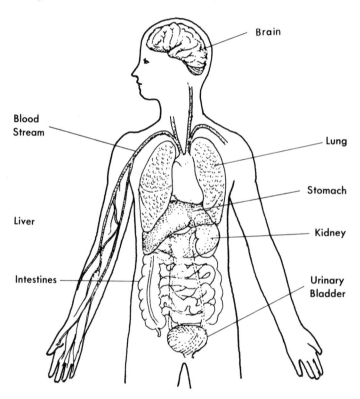

produce more noticeable effects on the body. The drinker's speech may become slurred, he may stagger, and may have trouble focusing his eyes. As still more alcohol is consumed (five to six drinks), the drinker has difficulty in accomplishing anything that requires coordination and may need help in walking. If more alcohol is consumed, the person may pass out.

A person who has consumed too much alcohol for his system experiences the effects while he is drinking and in fact until the alcohol has been removed from his body. He may also feel the effects the next morning. This is usually called a hangover, and its symptoms are headache, vomiting, loss of appetite, and fatigue.

87. How does alcohol affect the brain?

When alcohol is consumed, it goes almost directly to the bloodstream, affecting the central nervous system. A small amount of alcohol relaxes a person and makes him less tense. As the person continues to drink, his mental functions become depressed. The ability to think, reason, and remember is impaired, as is the ability to make decisions. Emotions such as love, hate, and fear are also intensified. If the person continues drinking, the senses (hearing, seeing, touching, tasting, and smelling) become befuddled.

Since the brain is also the control point for the voluntary and automatic motor functions of the body, these are also affected by alcohol. The degree to which these functions are affected depends on the amount of alcohol consumed. When small amounts of alcohol are consumed, the motor functions are not noticeably affected. However, larger amounts result in quite obvious effects.

88. Does alcohol make a person warmer?

One of the initial feelings a person experiences after consuming a small amount of alcohol is the sensation of warmth. Since alcohol dilates the peripheral blood vessels, it temporarily provides a sense of warmth. However, alcohol does not raise the body's temperature; it actually lowers it.

89. Does alcohol make a person stronger?

Alcohol does not make a person stronger. Since one of the initial effects of a small amount of alcohol is exhilaration and stimulation, it is quite possible that a person feels better or stronger. Also, as was noted in discussing alcohol's effects on the brain, more than a small amount of alcohol can dull a person's judgment. A person who has been drinking may feel that he can perform physical feats that he otherwise could not accomplish. Yet this would not be the case; not only does alcohol not increase strength, but it can impair coordination, causing even simple tasks to become more difficult.

90. Does alcohol make a person braver?

Alcohol may very well make a person feel braver. One of the main reasons given by adults and teen-agers for alcohol use is that it helps them be sociable. In effect, this implies that they would not be as comfortable in a social situation without having a small amount of alcohol. Alcohol may indeed make these people braver in the sense that they are more comfortable and at ease.

Though alcohol is not the cause of crimes against property such as stealing, it is often used to release inhibitions and relieve tensions once these crimes are planned. Crimes that are attributable to alcohol are mostly crimes of bodily assault. That is, alcohol has dulled an intoxicated person's judgment and enabled him to hurt another person—something he probably would not do in a sober state. Examples of this might be a businessman taking a swing at his boss because of a political disagreement or an intoxicated husband beating his wife or children.

91. Does alcohol help a person relax?

Yes, a small amount of alcohol does relax a person, relieve tension, and release inhibitions. Due to these effects, alcohol is used by people to enjoy a party, to enable them to sleep, or to relax after work.

92. Does alcohol stimulate the appetite?

Yes, a small quantity of alcohol stimulates the secretion of gastric juice in the stomach, which in turn increases the appetite. However, larger amounts of alcohol may cause a loss of appetite.

93. What does the body do with alcohol?

When beverage alcohol is consumed, most of it flows into the stomach via the digestive system. The drinker does not feel the effects of alcohol while it is in the stomach. However, some alcohol is absorbed into the bloodstream through the walls of the stomach. The remaining alcohol passes into the small intestine, where it also is absorbed into the bloodstream. Once the alcohol is in the bloodstream it circulates throughout the body. In its path of circulation in the blood, the alcohol reaches the brain and the drinker begins to feel the effects of alcohol (i.e., sensation of warmth, relaxation). If only a small amount of alcohol (about ½ oz. per hour) is consumed, the person will feel only slight effects; however, if more alcohol is consumed, the effects will be more noticeable.

94. How does the body get rid of alcohol?

Alcohol is eliminated by the body in two ways: elimination and oxidation. The process of elimination removes only about 10 percent of the alcohol. A small amount travels to the lungs (via the bloodstream), where it evaporates into the air and is exhaled. Another small amount of alcohol is removed from the blood by the kidneys, from which it is passed out of the body in urine.

Approximately 90 percent of the alcohol consumed is removed from the body by oxidation. Oxidation means to unite a substance with oxygen, and most of the oxidation of alcohol takes place in the liver. Since the liver can oxidize only a small amount of alcohol at one time, the remaining alcohol leaves the liver unchanged and continues to circulate in the body to return to the liver for oxidation. Each time alcohol enters the liver, a portion of it is changed into a substance known as acetaldehyde; this substance combines with oxygen (oxidation) to produce acetic acid and water. The acetic acid is then oxidized (united with oxygen) to produce water and carbon dioxide.

The process of oxidation continues until all the alcohol has been removed from the body. The approximate times for various amounts of alcohol to leave the body are given in question 96.

95. Does the body's oxidation of alcohol produce calories?

Oxidation of alcohol by the body does produce calories. An ounce of alcohol contains approximately 163 calories

(105 calories in a 1½-oz. glass of whisky, a 5-oz. glass of wine, or a 12-oz. glass of beer). Though alcohol contains calories, it does not contain the vitamins and other nutrients provided by food.

96. How long does it take the body to get rid of alcohol?

Since about 90 percent of the alcohol consumed leaves the body by the process of oxidation, it should be noted that the liver, which plays a major role in the oxidation process, can oxidize only a certain amount of alcohol per hour. In a person weighing approximately 160 lbs. the oxidation rate is about 7 grams of alcohol per hour. That is, about ¾ oz. of distilled spirits or 2½ oz. of wine or 6 oz. of beer can be oxidized by the body in one hour. If a 160-lb. person drank ¾ oz. of distilled spirits, or 2½ oz. of wine, or 6 oz. of beer per hour, the alcohol would never accumulate in the body and only very slight effects of alcohol (a slight feeling of exhilaration) would be felt. If more than this amount is consumed, the effects of alcohol become more noticeable and the time required for alcohol to leave the body is as follows:

---

1 drink*———— 2 hours
2 drinks———— 4 hours
4 drinks———— 8 hours
5 drinks————10 hours

   * A drink is defined here as 1½ oz. of distilled spirit, or 5 oz. of wine, or 12 oz. of beer.

---

97. Can alcohol affect one's health?

The answer to this question is yes and no. In most cases, it depends on how much a person drinks and how often.

There is a certain small percentage of people (those with liver problems) whose health would be affected by even a small amount of alcohol. However, most people can drink moderately or on an occasional basis with no adverse effects on their health. People who often drink large amounts of alcoholic beverages develop health problems related to alcohol. When we consider an alcoholic (alcoholism is explained in question 128), alcohol is extremely harmful to that person's health and well-being.

98. What does Blood Alcohol Concentration (BAC) mean?

Blood Alcohol Concentration (BAC) is the amount of alcohol present in a person's blood; it is always written as part of a percent. The BAC and related number of drinks for a person of approximately 160 lb. is as follows:

EFFECTS OF ALCOHOL ON THE HUMAN BODY

Number of Drinks*	Blood Alcohol Concentration
1	0.03%
2	0.06%
3	0.09%
4	0.12%
5	0.15%

* A drink is defined as 1½ oz. of distilled spirit, 5 oz. of wine, or 12 oz. of beer.

The chart provided for question 80 also relates the BAC to the effects of alcohol on the body and the time required for alcohol to leave the body.

99. What is responsible drinking?

Responsibility is defined as the ability "to respond or answer for one's conduct and obligations" (Webster's Third International Dictionary). Responsible drinking is the use of alcohol in an accountable manner; that is, the person is able to answer for his actions and obligations and in no way causes harm to himself or others.

100. Is light or moderate drinking harmful?

Light or moderate drinking is not harmful to most people in most situations. However, there are certain persons for whom any drinking may be harmful, for instance, a recovering alcoholic or a person with a liver problem.

101. How much alcohol can a person drink without becoming drunk?

A person who weighs 160 lb. can drink approximately ¾ oz. of distilled spirits, 2½ oz. of wine, or 6 oz. of beer per hour. This is approximately half the normal size drink of the various beverages. To avoid having the alcohol accumulate in the body, the person could drink a normal size drink at two-hour intervals. If a person drinks more than this amount of alcohol in a shorter time, he begins to feel the effects of alcohol.

102. Can you drink without getting drunk?

Absolutely. A person can drink slowly and spread his drinking over a period of time and not get drunk. However, people who cannot control their drinking and become intoxicated every time they drink may have an alcohol problem.

103. Is it necessary to serve food if one is serving drinks?

Serving food along with beverage alcohol is an absolute must, just as it is a sound practice to eat before drinking. When food is eaten as one drinks, it slows the process by which the alcohol is absorbed into the bloodstream, somewhat slowing the effects alcohol has on the human body.

104. What kinds of food should be served at a party where alcohol is served?

The best types of food to serve are ones that contain protein—cheese, meats, etc. If one serves only snack foods that make people thirsty, they may consume more alcohol than they intended.

105. Are there some hints for serving alcoholic beverages at a party to minimize problems related to alcohol use?

There are some very helpful hints for serving alcohol with a minimum of problems. They are:

1. Serve appetizing and appealing nonalcoholic beverages as well as alcoholic ones. Punch, soft drinks, and juices should be available as alternatives for guests who don't drink as well as for drinkers who feel they've had enough but still want a glass to hold.

2. Food should always accompany the serving of alcohol. The best types of snacks are pieces of cheese, small chunks of meat (hot dogs, meatballs, etc.), and cream or cheese dips. These slow the rate at which alcohol is absorbed into the

bloodstream. Salty snacks such as peanuts, chips, and pretzels tend to make the drinker thirsty and may motivate him to drink more. If salty snacks are to be served, an accompanying dip is a must.

3. Make sure that the amount of alcoholic beverage for a drink is measured, either by a measuring device on the bottle or yourself. This assures the host and guest that the amount of alcohol in a drink is the desired and expected amount. A person can metabolize about a 12-oz. beer, a 5-oz. glass of wine or 1½ oz. of hard liquor in about two hours. If more alcohol is put into the drink, the person who is spacing drinks so as not to become intoxicated may wind up drunk without knowing why.

4. Since time enables the body to eliminate alcohol, people should feel free to space their drinks. It is not hospitable always to make sure a guest's glass is full. Often a guest winds up with an unwanted drink simply to avoid refusing the host.

5. Close the bar about an hour to an hour and a half before the party is to end. During this time, cake and coffee or other nonalcoholic beverages should be served. Though it is not the coffee or the food that return a guest to a sober state, the additional time it takes to serve and consume them may do the trick.

6. Never serve "one for the road." It takes about 20 minutes for the alcohol in a drink to be absorbed into the bloodstream and the person to feel the effects of that drink. A person who was not intoxicated at the party's end but has "one for the road" may wind up in no condition to drive home.

7. If your best efforts are subverted and a guest

becomes intoxicated, do not let him or her drive. Persuade the guest to let someone else drive, call a cab, arrange for a ride with a friend, drive the guest's car yourself, or let him or her spend the night at your home. Though people sometimes act as if it's unmanly to relinquish their keys, this is a misguided ego trip and one that, if allowed, can fill a host with guilt for the rest of his life.

8. Bear in mind throughout the party that enjoying friends is the primary goal; it is not to see how much alcohol can be served or consumed. Since no one enjoys an intoxicated person, it is a host's responsibility to assure that alcohol is consumed without problems by the guests and for the guests.

Chapter VII

Alcohol Problems

106. What does being "high" mean?

High is a state produced by consumption of alcohol. The person is obviously affected by the alcohol (e.g., gay or drowsy) yet is not drunk or offensive.

107. What does being "tight" mean?

Tight is a degree of intoxication (more intoxicated than high but less than drunk). A person who is "tight" has slurred speech, unsteady walk, and may be nauseated.

108. What does it mean to be drunk?

Drunk, intoxicated, and inebriated are all words used to describe a person whose ability to function mentally and physically is significantly impaired because of consumption of alcohol. Usually a person who becomes so impaired experiences a hangover the following day.

109. At what Blood Alcohol Concentration is a person considered drunk or intoxicated?

A Blood Alcohol Concentration of .10 percent (approximately three to four drinks within an hour) produces a person whose judgment is cloudy, whose decision-making ability is reduced, and who has poor physical coordination. Such a person is considered to be "under the

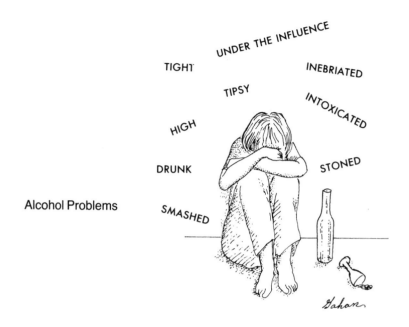

UNDER THE INFLUENCE

TIGHT

INEBRIATED

TIPSY

INTOXICATED

HIGH

DRUNK

STONED

Alcohol Problems

SMASHED

influence." At the level of .10 percent the person is considered legally drunk and may be charged with driving while intoxicated.

110.   Can a person become drunk just drinking beer?

A person can become drunk from drinking too much of any beverage that contains alcohol. Beer contains alcohol; there is approximately the same amount of alcohol in a 12-oz. can of beer, a 5-oz. glass of wine, and 1½ oz. of hard liquor.

111.   Does how much you weigh have anything to do with how much you can drink without getting drunk?

After an alcoholic beverage is consumed it flows into the stomach. Some of the alcohol is absorbed directly into the bloodstream, and the rest passes into the small intestine. Most of the alcohol is absorbed from the small intestine into the bloodstream to circulate throughout the body. A person who weighs more has more blood and body fluids into which alcohol is dispersed; therefore, a larger person will have a lower concentration of alcohol in the blood than a smaller person who has consumed the same amount.

The myth about a person who can "hold his liquor" or "drink everyone under the table" is exploded by the relationship of weight and the effects of alcohol. A heavier person can obviously consume more alcohol than a smaller one because of the larger amount of body fluid through which the alcohol can be dispersed.

112. What does driving while "impaired" mean?

A person who is impaired by alcohol usually exhibits a reduced ability to spot hazards and react to danger, a decreased ability to adapt to day/night light changes, and tunnel vision (a narrow scope of vision). These factors result in a six to seven times greater accident risk potential than in an alcohol-free driver.

113. What does "under the influence" mean?

"Under the influence" refers to a level of intoxication that is usually set at a Blood Alcohol Concentration of .10 percent; it is also referred to in some areas as "driving while intoxicated." When discussed in terms of driving, the person who is "under the influence" often exhibits gross impairment of skills and judgment, double vision, and conspicuous intoxication that result in an extremely high accident risk potential. The risk of causing a crash becomes 25 times as great as it is for the alcohol-free person.

114. How much alcohol does an adult have to drink to become drunk?

A person with a Blood Alcohol Concentration of .10 percent is considered to be legally drunk in most states. For a 160-lb. person this means that approximately three to four drinks have been consumed in a short period of time (approximately one hour). The effects of alcohol on a person depend on many factors, including the size of the drinker, the size of the drink, the time during which alcohol is consumed, experience with drinking, and whether there is food in the stomach.

115. How much alcohol will make a teen-ager drunk?

Most teen-agers become intoxicated on less alcohol than it would take to make an adult drunk. This is due to many reasons:

1. A teen-ager's body is usually smaller in size and weight than an adult's body. Therefore the percentage of alcohol compared with the volume of blood is higher.
2. A teen-ager has less experience drinking than an adult does. One drink is apt to make a young person dizzy, whereas one drink may only increase an adult's appetite or bring slight relaxation.
3. A teen-ager expects alcohol to provide certain feelings or changes in behavior. Since alcohol tends to intensify a mood, a young person who expects to get giddy or high from alcohol will most probably achieve this state.

This explanation has not specifically answered the question of how much alcohol will make a young person drunk. It has not been given to avoid an answer, but rather to explain the difficulty in stating a specific amount of alcohol that will make a teen-ager drunk. A 13-year-old who is having his or her first drink at a party may become intoxicated on a glass of wine, whereas a 17-year-old youth who has had some experience with alcoholic beverages, has eaten, and does not expect alcohol to make him drunk may be able to consume 3 glasses of wine in six hours and feel the effects only slightly.

116. What is "switching drinks"?

"Switching drinks" refers to changing the type of beverage alcohol consumed on a specific drinking occasion, for instance, a drink containing scotch to one containing rye, or beer to wine.

117. Does one get sick or drunk from switching drinks?

Many people believe that switching the type of alcoholic beverage consumed causes them to become intoxicated, get sick, or develop a hangover the next morning. It is the amount of alcohol consumed, *not the type of beverage*, that causes a person to become intoxicated, get sick, or develop a hangover. However, people who switch drinks may inadvertently drink more than intended and therefore experience problems related to the increased amount.

118. What is a hangover?

A hangover is the result of a person's drinking an excess amount of alcoholic beverages. The effects of this over-consumption are fatigue, headache, nausea, and feelings of guilt and depression.

119. How do you get rid of a hangover?

There are many ineffective "cures" for a hangover. Some of them are tomato juice, black coffee, and raw egg in juice. Some people do obtain some relief from the un-pleasantness of a hangover when they follow one of the "cures," yet the relief is only partial and occurs mainly because they believe in it. There are actually only two ways to get rid of a hangover. The first, a high-risk method, which does eliminate some of the symptoms of a hangover, is to drink more alcohol; however, this can lead to a person's overindulging again and incurring another hangover. Thus a cycle of drinking can be created that is very difficult to break. The other method, a low-risk sure cure for a hangover, is time. When the body is given time to eliminate all the alcohol accumulated in it, the hangover will disappear.

120. How does a person who is intoxicated become sober?

Just as there are many so-called cures for a hangover, there are many so-called quick methods to sober up an intoxicated person. Some of these are coffee, a brisk walk, and physical exercise. Unfortunately, these methods do not help an intoxicated person become less intoxicated; they do produce a wide-awake drunk who can be more dangerous than a sleepy one. There is only one known way for a person to become sober; that is, to stop drinking and give the body time to eliminate the alcohol.

Though most sobering-up methods are myths, they have produced some excellent customs. The common practice of ending a party or get-together where beverage alcohol has been served with coffee and cake is based on the myth that coffee helps to make a person sober. The coffee does not make a person sober, yet the time period in which the coffee and cake are served is most beneficial. Since time alone aids the body in removing the alcohol and its effects, any device used to provide a nondrinking period after consumption of alcoholic beverages is useful.

121. Can you get sick or die from too much alcohol?

Yes, a person can get sick and die from too much alcohol. A hangover, described in question 118, is certainly a sick state, caused by consuming too much alcohol.

Usually a person can consume only a certain amount of alcohol before passing out (that is, more than a pint of whisky or its equivalent to produce a BAC of about .30 to .40 percent). A person who has consumed enough alcohol to have lost consciousness is not able to drink more. However, if a person were to quickly drink about a quart of whisky before passing out, not only would unconsciousness result, but the Blood Alcohol Concentration would reach between .50 percent (state of deep coma) and 1 percent (death). As the BAC nears 1 percent, the breathing center of the brain becomes paralyzed and death occurs.

Chapter VIII

Alcoholism: Disease and Treatment

122. What is an alcohol problem?

An alcohol problem results from the misuse of beverage alcohol. This misuse can occur for the reasons for which a person drinks (e.g., to forget a problem, to get through the day, to escape). Alcohol problems can also occur when a person continually consumes an excess of alcohol and reaches an intoxicated state. Also, any use of alcohol that results in harm to the drinker or others is considered an alcohol problem.

123. What is problem drinking?

Problem drinking is the abuse or misuse of alcohol that causes problems for the drinker or others. It is estimated that there are 4 million problem drinkers in the U.S. today; this number does not include the approximately 6 million alcoholics. Problem drinking occurs for inappropriate reasons and is marked by continual heavy use of alcohol. Many theorists believe that problem drinkers have actually entered an early phase of alcoholism and should seek treatment.

124. How does a person know if he is a problem drinker?

A person who is having problems related to alcohol use,

increasing the consumption of alcohol, and drinking more often than usual is exhibiting signs of problem drinking.

125. What are the symptoms of problem drinking?

The National Institute on Alcohol Abuse and Alcoholism has developed the following simple questions to help determine if a person has a "drinking problem."

1. Do you think and talk about drinking often?
2. Do you drink more now than you used to?
3. Do you sometimes gulp drinks?
4. Do you often take a drink to help you relax?
5. Do you drink when you are alone?
6. Do you sometimes forget what happened when you were drinking?
7. Do you keep a bottle hidden somewhere at home or at work for a quick "pick-me-up"?
8. Do you need a drink to have fun?
9. Do you ever start drinking without really thinking about it?
10. Do you ever drink in the morning to relieve a hangover?

126. Can a teen-ager be a problem drinker?

Yes, there are teen-agers who are problem drinkers. Research studies indicate that of approximately 70 percent of the teenage drinking population, 5 percent have problems related to their alcohol use. In the majority of these problems alcohol is a contributing factor (drinking and driving, vandalism, etc.). About 2 percent of this group can be identified as having specific alcohol problems, such as drinking alone or drinking in the morning.

127. What should you do if one of your parents is a problem drinker?

First you must realize that you are not the cause of your parent's drinking problem and that there is probably little that you can do to stop it. Second you must try to understand why your parent is drinking in such a manner and discuss the problem with your non-problem-drinking parent. Often that parent attempts to cover up or gloss over the difficulties of the problem drinker; knowing that you are aware of the problem may help him or her to discuss it. A supportive adult (a teacher, a member of the clergy, a doctor) outside of the family may also be able to help. Alateen, an organization of teen-agers with an alcoholic parent, would be eager to help you understand this problem.

128. What is alcoholism?

Mark Keller has clearly defined alcoholism as "a chronic disease manifested by repeated implicative drinking so as to cause injury to the drinker's health or to his social or economic functioning."[1]

Alcoholism is a chronic and progressive illness; it is chronic because it is long-lasting (that is, most alcoholics are not able to return to social drinking); it is progressive because its symptoms develop in stages and create a problem in a major life area, such as work or family.

129. Is alcoholism a disease?

Yes, alcoholism is a disease just as tuberculosis and heart disease are diseases. For many years it was believed that

---

[1] Keller, M. *The Definition of Alcoholism.* New Brunswick, NJ: Rutgers Center of Alcohol Studies, 1960.

alcoholics were weak-willed persons with flawed characters. This kind of thinking was and is very harmful for two reasons: (1) the family of an alcoholic constantly covered up his or her alcohol problem because of embarassment, and (2) the alcoholic would not or could not admit his problem and therefore seek treatment. Since we now know that alcoholism is a disease and society accepts it as such, it is easier for the alcoholic to seek treatment, for the family to admit the problem and seek help, and for more and varied treatment programs to flourish.

130. Why is alcoholism called an illness?

Alcoholism is characterized by dependence on alcohol. It interferes with the person's health, family and social life, and economic functioning. Like other diseases, it usually requires some type of treatment to enable the person to recover.

131. What are the phases of alcoholism?

There are four phases of alcoholism that usually take five to seven years to develop. It must be remembered that these phases are not always in the same order or always gone through by an alcoholic. However, they are useful to describe the behavior and symptoms of the progressive stages through which most alcoholics pass.

The first stage is called the warning stage. It occurs when the drinker uses alcohol as a drug to relieve tension and to feel good. During this stage the person's drinking pattern changes from occasional or frequent to regular or daily, and he/she seeks more and more occasions and reasons to drink. He/she consumes more alcohol on each drinking occasion and begins to build a tolerance to alcohol in this stage.

The second stage of alcoholism is the danger stage. The drinker needs alcohol in larger quantities to obtain relief. Deeper and more frequent intoxication, as well as the sneaking of drinks, are part of this phase. Other symptoms are drinking alone, gulping drinks, blackouts (inability to remember something that occurred during or after drinking), guilt feelings about drinking habits, and occasional loss of time from work because of drinking.

The crucial phase is the third stage of alcoholism. In this phase the drinker loses control when he/she begins drinking and drinks more than intended. The drinker now makes detailed excuses for drinking, always managing to blame others. He/she blacks out more frequently, gets noticeably intoxicated, behaves aggressively especially toward those he/she blames, and withdraws from social interaction. Neglect of responsibilities, extravagant spending, and protection of liquor supply by hiding (if necessary) are also symptoms of this stage. The drinker may require hospitalization at this point for a physical illness related to alcohol consumption.

The fourth and last stage of alcoholism is the chronic stage, during which the alcoholic may be intoxicated most of the time. During this stage the alcoholic has completely lost control of his/her drinking and will drink anything (even rubbing alcohol) that will intoxicate regardless of the harm these substances may do to the body. The alcoholic finds sobriety a torment and finally gives up the alibi system for drinking. He/she may also experience bodily shaking, which prevents performance of very simple functions such as tying a shoe or shaving. At this point, the alcoholic either seeks help or goes under.

PHASES OF ALCOHOLISM

Phase 1:
- Uses alcohol to relieve tension;
- Seeks more drinking occasions and drinks more often;
- Changes friends to accommodate heavier drinking;
- Builds tolerance to alcohol.

Phase 2:
- Craves alcohol;
- Requires larger amounts of alcohol;
- Seeks deeper and more frequent intoxication;
- Sneaks drinks;
- Blacks out (period of temporary amnesia);
- Experiences guilt feelings.

Phase 3:
- Rationalizes drinking;
- Loses control once drinking begins;
- Blacks out frequently;
- Becomes conspicuously and frequently intoxicated;
- Behaves aggressively;
- Withdraws from family and social environment;
- Drinks in the morning occasionally;
- Withdraws from responsibilities;
- Is hospitalized.

Phases 4:
- Loses control over the use of alcohol;
- Drinks often, or every day, in the morning;
- Drinks to intoxication;
- Goes on benders;
- Experiences torment when sober;
- Drinks any form of alcohol;
- Relinguishes the alibi system for drinking (rationalization);
- Goes under or seeks help.

132. What is a blackout?

A blackout is a loss of memory of events (total or in part) that occurred during a drinking session or immediately after drinking. It is an amnesia that is not combined with a loss of consciousness. A drinker may seem to others to be acting normally during and after drinking but on the next day be completely unable to recall parts of the evening, such as a conversation with another guest or getting home from the party.

133. What causes alcoholism?

Alcoholism is a complex problem, for which there is no one known cause. Many theories are being researched to attempt to isolate the causes of this illness. One theory is that alcoholism is hereditary and runs in the family like color blindness or baldness. Another theory is that alcohol is a habit-forming drug, and still another theory involves a relationship between alcoholism and blood-sugar levels. There is also a theory that some people are prone to addiction because of a physical predisposition. Another theory is that the causes of alcoholism are psychological; that is, the use of alcohol to solve problems may result in dependence on alcohol and progress to alcoholism.

134. Is alcoholism hereditary?

Theorists are studying the possibility that alcoholism runs in families because a disproportionate number of people who had an alcoholic parent become alcoholic them-selves. It must be noted that another disproportionately high percentage of alcoholics come from abstinent homes; but children from abstinent homes are often descendants of alcoholics, and therefore both groups would tend to prove the heredity theory.

135. Can a person who drinks only wine or only beer be an alcoholic?

Yes, wine and beer contain alcohol, and a person need only be dependent upon alcohol to create problems for himself and others and progress to becoming an alcoholic.

136. What is an alcoholic?

An alcoholic is a person who suffers from the disease of alcoholism. An alcoholic may be male or female, young or old, rich or poor, white or black, professional or working man. Just as there is no one reason why a person becomes an alcoholic, there is also not one type of alcoholic person. However, there are a few generalizations common to most alcoholics. An alcoholic usually lives in an unreal world, is often immature and self-conscious, and requires a feeling of superiority. Though alcoholics usually remain with their families in home situations, they do break away from their group of friends and often avoid family gatherings.

137. What kind of people become alcoholics?

Alcoholism affects persons of both sexes and all races, socioeconomic levels, and religious beliefs. There is no one type of people who become alcoholics. Alcoholics are found in leadership positions as well as among the jobless.

138. How does a person know if he/she is an alcoholic?

Alcoholism is a progressive disease; it usually takes between five and seven years to fully develop its hold on the victim. During this time a person may not be aware of or willing to admit having problems with alcohol. The following questions are presented to highlight some of the noticeable symptoms of problem drinking or an early stage of alcoholism. There is no key by which to rate the questions. They are not meant to diagnose a condition, but rather to highlight some symptoms of a problem and heighten a person's awareness if a problem exists.

- Do you drink alone?
- Do you sneak a drink in the morning?
- Do you ever feel that you need a drink?
- Do you become irritable when drinking?
- Do you drink to get drunk?
- Has your drinking harmed your family or friends in any way?
- Does drinking change your personality, creating an entirely new you?
- Are you more impulsive when you are drinking?
- Do you have to drink to enjoy social functions?
- Does drinking make you moody?
- Have you ever blacked out (lost your memory of what you did) while drinking?
- Has drinking hurt your reputation?

139. Can a teen-ager be an alcoholic?

Yes, there are teen-agers who are alcoholics; however, this is a very small and as yet undocumented part of the teen-age drinking population. Obviously, these young people are part of the group (discussed in question 79) that has problems directly related to alcohol. Unfortunately, this group of young people are often "troubled teens"; that is, they have a variety of complex problems and seek escape through alcohol or other substances. Alcoholism usually takes between five and seven years to develop. This would mean that a person had to be problem drinking between the ages of 10 and 12. Though this has happened in some instances, it is not common. What is more common, perhaps, is that teen-agers combine other substances with alcohol and do not go through the traditional phases or the normal period of alcoholism development. Alcoholism that develops in this manner is still alcoholism. Again, however, it must be mentioned that we are discussing a very small group of teen-agers, and that of this group, most are troubled teens.

140. Are people who drink every day alcoholics?

Persons who drink every day may or may not be alcoholic. There are people who drink wine with dinner every evening who are not alcoholics. There are also alcoholics who do not drink every day.

141. Why do people become alcoholics?

There is no one cause of alcoholism. Alcoholism is a complex disease that may have a variety of causes. Since most alcoholics were able to drink moderately at one time, there is no way to recognize a future alcoholic when he or she is growing up or drinking moderately. There are no tests that can be given to ascertain if young person is at risk of becoming an alcoholic. It is not until the symptoms of alcoholism become apparent that it is recognizable.

142. What is the cost to society of alcoholism?

The cost of alcoholism to society is extremely high. It is estimated that one alcoholic directly affects the lives of at least three other persons. In the U.S. the number of alcoholics is approximately 6 million,[2] with an additional 4 million people considered problem drinkers. When this number is multiplied by three, the result is approximately 30 million people directly affected by alcohol problems. This represents a significant cost to our society. The cost of alcoholism can also be calculated financially. It is conservatively estimated that alcohol problems cost the nation as a whole over $50 billion a year. Though this figure represents only the dollar cost of alcoholism to society, it demonstrates the costliness of this disease.

143. How can an alcoholic stop drinking?

Many types of treatment are available to an alcoholic who desires help. In most cases an alcoholic requires some type of treatment or help to be able to stop drinking. It is a rare phenomenon when an alcoholic decides to stop drinking and does so without any assistance.

144. Why don't alcoholics just stop drinking?

Alcoholics don't just stop drinking because their bodies have built up a need for alcohol. Alcohol has also become a way of life for the alcoholic; he is dependent on alcohol and requires it in order to function. This is not to imply that alcoholics can't stop drinking. It is meant to provide understanding of the difficulty that a life without alcohol presents to the alcoholic. This is why in most cases physical and emotional assistance is necessary to help an alcoholic recover from his disease.

[2] This estimate of the number of alcoholics in the U.S. is based on a formula developed by E.M. Jellinek and is presented in Hyman, M.M., Zimmermann, M.A., Gurioli, C. and Helrich, A., *Drinkers, Drinking and Alcohol-Related Mortality and Hospitalizations: A Statistical Compendium.* New Brunswick, NJ: Rutgers Center of Alcohol Studies, 1980.

145. Are alcoholics "skid-row bums"?

The idea that most alcoholics are skid-row bums wandering around begging money to buy a drink has been one of the most harmful myths surrounding alcoholism. Only about 5 percent of all the people with drinking problems are living on skid row; the others remain at home and continue to work. The skid-row stereotype has been harmful in two ways: (1) it has caused alcoholics and their families to cover up the problem because of the terrible image conjured up by the word alcoholic; and (2) it has provided an unrealistic rationale for alcoholics and their families who won't admit their problem. In effect, the alcoholic says: "I can't be an alcoholic because I'm not a bum, I live at home, I go to work." Consequently, many alcoholics do not seek early treatment for their disease, nor do their families seek understanding of it. This is unfortunate because the earlier the disease is treated, the easier and faster the person can return to normal functioning.

146. What is the average age of alcoholics?

Most alcoholics show symptoms of their illness between 35 and 45, although there are younger as well as older alcoholics.

147. Do people die of alcoholism?

The effects on the body of years of alcoholism may indeed be deadly. Deaths due to cirrhosis of the liver[3] (impairment of the liver function as well as the circulation of

---

[3] Although people other than alcoholics can have cirrhosis of the liver, the percentage of such cases is relatively small. The majority of persons who have cirrhosis are alcoholics.

blood and the flow of bile from this organ) is one method of calculating the number of alcoholics. Other alcoholics may suffer from diseases caused by vitamin deficiencies because they have not eaten properly for years. Physical diseases caused by vitamin deficiency are beriberi, pellegra, and polyneuropathy. Mental disorders are also often related to alcoholism, such as alcohol psychosis, delirium tremens, Korsakoff's psychosis, and Wernicke's disease.

148. Where can a person obtain help for an alcohol problem?

There are many types of people from whom an alcoholic can obtain help. Doctors, members of the clergy, or community health or social workers can help an alcoholic seek treatment. Most hospitals have inpatient or outpatient clinics to aid alcoholics. There are also public and private hospitals exclusively designed for the treatment of alcoholism. Alcoholics Anonymous (AA), a self-help organization for persons who desire to stop drinking, is listed in the phone book. AA is a nonsectarian fellowship that was established in 1935 by two alcoholics. Its aim is to provide an opportunity for alcoholics to become abstinent. It has no constitution, no membership list, and no dues. Alcoholics Anonymous requires only that an alcoholic desire to stop drinking and be willing to seek help from a power greater than the self.

Help is also available for the family of an alcoholic. Al-Anon family groups were established by and for spouses of alcoholics. Al-Anon is patterned very closely after Alcoholics Anonymous; these groups hold open and closed meetings, are self-supporting, and avoid public identification of their members. Al-Anon members may have spouses who no longer drink or who are still drinking. Al-Anon groups function to help members deal with their alcoholic spouse's problems and their own during the time that the spouse is drinking and also when he/she is sober. Alateen groups were established for the teen-age children of alcoholics to help these young people understand the disease of alcoholism and their alcoholic parents. These groups are open to young people whose alcoholic parent is or is not a member of AA.

149. What types of treatment are used to help alcoholics recover from alcoholism?

A variety of treatment services and facilities are available to alcoholics. The first step in any treatment program is detoxification, which is the elimination of alcohol from the body. Detoxification usually takes place in a medical facility, because the person can experience severe reactions during withdrawal from alcohol. After detoxification a combination medical and psychiatric approach may be used. Private and public hospitals often provide the treatment setting. Treatment can be accomplished in an inpatient or outpatient setting or a combination, depending on the needs of the alcoholic. Drugs such as Antabuse or Temposil are often used in this method to produce a physical reaction to alcohol; a person who is taking one of these drugs and consumes alcohol reacts with nausea. Individual or group psychiatric consultation as well as counseling are often used as methods of treatment for alcoholics. Halfway houses, another type of treatment facility, create a bridge for the person between hospitalization and a return to full responsibilities. A resident of a halfway house works daily and may visit his family; however, he returns for sleeping and eating to the halfway house. Thus the person begins to function and gain independence in an atmosphere that fosters sobriety.

Outpatient clinics, usually a part of a general hospital, are another type of treatment. The person receives medical or psychiatric treatment on a regular basis but is not hospitalized.

Some industries also offer in-house counseling programs for alcoholic employees.

150. Can an alcoholic be helped to recover from alcoholism?

Yes, an alcoholic can be helped to recover from alcoholism. Recovery is not called a cure, because an alcoholic cannot resume normal drinking again. However, by remaining abstinent, he/she is able to function and live life fully once again.

The following are suggested guidelines for family members of the alcoholic:

- Learn as much as you can about alcohol and its use.
- Obtain information about alcoholism.
- Think about your feelings about the disease of alcoholism.
- Try to understand how the alcoholic in your family is affecting your life.
- Attend meetings of Al-Anon or Alateen to learn from the experiences of others.
- Discuss the situation with a trusted person such as a doctor or clergyman or a professional counselor.
- Maintain a healthy and happy atmosphere in the home.
- Remember that you are not the cause of the problem and that alcoholism is a disease from which individuals can recover.

Rehabilitation and treatment of an alcoholic can be accomplished in a variety of ways (see question #149). The alcoholic's family and its attitudes can set the stage for the process of treatment and rehabilitation by supportively dealing with the person and the problems related to alcoholism.

Chapter IX

Alcoholism: The Family Illness

The major stress of *Coping with Alcohol* has been on alcohol and your feelings about its use. The content questions about alcohol problems and alcoholism were presented to provide information on all aspects of alcohol and also to enable you to understand what an alcohol problem is and to realize that help is available.

Although the majority of people who drink don't have problems with their use of the substance, there are about 6 million alcoholics and an additional 4 million problem drinkers in the U.S. today. If each of these individuals affects the lives of three other people, some 30 million lives are affected by an alcohol problem. Some estimates indicate that the number is higher, and that 50 million individuals are affected. It is highly possible that you are now or will be affected by the alcoholism of a family member, spouse, friend, or working associate.

The impact of alcoholism on members of the alcoholic's family is significant but often ignored. Alcoholism is a *family illness*. This is not to say that every member of an alcoholic's family becomes alcoholic. Rather, it means that each person in the family is directly affected by the alcoholic member and his or her disease.

The alcoholic revolves his/her life around drinking, making excuses for drinking, or blaming others for making him or her drink so much. Feelings of guilt and remorse are interspersed between drinking experiences. Behavior often fluctuates between grandiose actions, aggression, and resentment. As the alcoholism develops, work and financial problems further add to the alcoholic's dilemma and increase the mood swings. Avoidance of family and friends, neglect of health, and deterioration of ability to function accompany lengthy periods of intoxication. Since the disease of alcoholism may take from five to seven years or longer to develop, turmoil in the home increases in intensity during this time.

The spouse often spends years in an attempt to hide the drinking problem from other family members, children, friends, and work associates. In the cover-up process, often called denial, the spouse also changes. The non-alcoholic begins to withdraw from social activities for fear the problem will be exposed, or just to "keep the peace" because the alcoholic refuses to associate with old friends or family—having found new drinking buddies. The spouse's social withdrawal is only part of what is happening. The spouse is also part of the cover-up and feels that this problem must be hidden at all costs. The spouse in effect may be controlled by the alcohol problem.

Feelings of stress, anxiety, and frustration also become part of the spouse's life. He or she may be hindered in day-to-day functioning, seeming to prefer or create upset. Though the nonalcoholic would like things the way they were, he/she is not able to stop the alcoholic's drinking. Added to this stressful situation is the mounting worry over financial matters, loss of job, effect on the children, and fear that ultimately everyone will know. The non-alcoholic spouse fluctuates between fighting about drinking and refusing to communicate with the alcoholic. Unfortunately these mood swings and stress also affect the children; even if children do not know what the problem is, they know that there is a problem.

The alcoholism has created a disorganization in the home and a lack of consistency. The children have also been withdrawn from family get-togethers and parties because their parents do not go. Of even greater significance is the fact that they do not know what they'll find when they come home. They may be greeted by the alcoholic parent in a drunken stupor, or by the non-alcoholic parent in an anxious and nontalkative mood, or by both parents acting OK. Each of these situations creates many problems. If the alcoholic is obviously intoxicated, the children will soon decide not to bring friends home and will withdraw from their peers. This, of course, makes the cover-up cycle complete in the family, as well as having a disastrous effect on the children's interaction with others. The situation of the nonalcoholic's anxiety and silence is also a severe problem for children, not only because of their inability to discuss the problem of one parent with the other, but also because the nonalcoholic parent is exhibiting problems also. The child begins to withdraw from this parent in hope of escaping the mood swings. Withdrawal is also seen as necessary because the nonalcoholic parent seems unpredictable. This unpredictability is the problem when everyone is having a better day and pretending to be OK. The children are relieved to experience this state, distrustful that it will last, and guilty that they can't make it last.

The guilt feeling of each family member in this system is extremely high. The alcoholic parent feels guilty because he/she can't or won't seek treatment, and the nonalcoholic parent feels guilty because of what is happening to the children and also for his or her role in the cover-up of the problem. The children feel guilty because they can't solve the problem; they often see themselves as the cause and aren't sure that they "like" either parent. Each family member has been directly affected by the alcoholism in the home, and each should seek counseling and help.

The alcoholic has many avenues of help and treatment. Treatment facilities are often located in general hospitals and provide inpatient or outpatient care or both. Some private facilities specialize in alcoholism treatment and rehabilitation, and groups of Alcoholics Anonymous are found throughout the world. It is important to note that even if the alcoholic refuses to acknowledge the disease and seek treatment, the other family members should seek help for themselves. If the alcoholic does seek help and begins to recover, many times the family members think that their problems are solved and don't seek help. This is unfortunate, because the effects of the alcoholism on each family member are significant. Each needs to learn about alcoholism, learn to deal with his or her feelings about what has happened, and learn to cope with the effects on his or her life.

Some persons who exhibit coping problems later in life are children of alcoholics who spent most of their lives trying to control their life-style, never having dealt with their tremendous sense of frustration in not being able to solve the problem in their home as they grew up. Covering up their sense of guilt and bottling up their emotions has only further aggravated their situation and minimized their coping skills. This is unfortunate and unnecessary. Help and understanding are available for children who are living with an alcoholic parent. Private counselors often specialize in family treatment or in counseling children of alcoholics. Alateen groups are also available in most areas and offer information, encourage-ment, and support. Teen-agers are welcome in Alateen groups even if their alcoholic parent does not belong to AA and their nonalcoholic parent is not a member of Al-Anon. Al-Anon is for spouses of alcoholics and offers information, help, guidance, and support.

Both Al-Anon and Alateen, as well as private thera-pists and counselors, endeavor to allow each family member to understand the role alcoholism has played in his or her life. Encouragement and techniques to moti-vate separation from the alcoholism while still being able to love the alcoholic spouse or parent are offered. The goal of seeking help is to knowledge the problems and deal with them now to enable each person to cope with life in the present and in the future.

Chapter **X**

Discussion of Drinking

Originally, I had intended to have two parts in this chapter, one for drinkers and one for nondrinkers. After thinking about it, I realized that this implied that the groups were basically different, which is not true. It also implied that a drinker is a drinker; that once a person identifies himself as a drinker, he/she will drink alcoholic beverages whenever they are served. The same applies to nondrinkers; a separate section indicated that this was a life decision, which may not be the case. The more I thought about this discussion section, the more I realized that the message is the same for all. *Use the knowledge and information you have learned, understand your feelings and attitudes, and make decisions that are best for your health and well-being.* This means that you must consider each specific occasion when alcohol is served and think about how you feel and what you must do to avoid high risks. This might mean that you choose not to drink on some occasions. It might also mean that you choose to limit the alcohol you consume at a party, especially if you are the driver. Hopefully, it will mean—for drinkers and nondrinkers alike—that you will be able to assert yourself regarding when you choose to drink, what you choose to drink, how much you choose to drink and why you choose to drink. As teen-agers become less ambivalent about alcohol, decide that pressure of any kind should not accompany use, and acknowledge each person's right to drink or not drink, society will have an excellent chance in the years to come to deal with alcohol and alcohol problems in a safe, sane, and humane manner.

Chapter **XI**

Adolescent Drug Use

Though the goals of *Coping with Alcohol* have been to provide information on alcohol and alcoholism and to motivate you to make responsible decisions about alcohol, it is not possible to ignore the prevalence of other drugs in the 1980's. This chapter on drug use in American society and among adolescents is offered to provide information and perspective on this most important issue.

The U.S. is drug-taking society. However, this is not the result of a collective conscious decision, nor is it understood or accepted by most people. As a society, we are comfortable with taking over-the-counter preparations to alleviate a wide range of discomforts. Weight control, headache relief, elimination of stomach distress, and aids for stress reduction are just a few of the items available in drugstores, in supermarkets, and in our medicine cabinets. It is interesting that the majority of Americans do not consider these over-the-counter products to be drugs.

Prescription medications also are often not thought of as drugs. Although users are aware that physician-ordered medications are drugs, they don't view their use of the medicine as drug-taking. Because medicines are intended to help us when we're sick and most often they actually do, they are categorized as good. Drug-taking has an implied negative image and is widely viewed as referring only to illegal or street drugs. However, it is estimated that every physician in the United States writes between five and ten thousand prescriptions a year. This high volume of medications indicates our acceptance of taking prescription drugs.

Our society seems to have difficulty in realizing that one can become dependent on over-the-counter products and prescribed medicines. It stems from our deep-seated conviction about good and bad drugs, our lack of knowledge regarding what is a drug, and our comfort in taking some types of substances. As a society, we are afraid of drugs and drug-taking; we think of these behaviors in negative concepts related to the drug scene of the 1960's. Words such as "addict" and "junkie" conjure visions of long-haired hippies, not the executive who is addicted to amphetamines or a minor tranquilizer. Unfortunately, the media emphasis on the drug-taking of the 1960's did not focus on society's attitude toward and use of drugs. We became very comfortable thinking of "them" and not "us" as the drug takers.

The lack of awareness of the substances we ingest, often the absence of thought before taking them, and the categorization of drugs as good and bad provide the societal background in which you, our adolescents, are raised. It is difficult for parents to share with their children thoughts and feelings about drug-taking if they are unable to acknowledge society's drug-taking behaviors. It is also difficult for parents to accept the fact that they often introduce the young to drugs and set the stage for a pattern of use.

When a child is born one of the first orders of business is to have the baby checked by a physician. During a child's early years medication is prescribed for a variety of ills: colic, fever, colds. As the child grows, not every ailment is taken to a physician for treatment. Some minor problems are handled by home remedies (e.g., chicken soup) or over-the-counter medication (e.g., cough medicine). By the time children have reached school age, most have taken prescriptions and over-the-counter medications.

Young people have also had learning experiences related to substances. They are aware that some substances are considered good and helpful and that many exist to eliminate discomfort; they also know how and for what reasons substances are used at home. However, they are often not aware that these substances are drugs and that their consumption initiates a pattern of substance use. It should not surprise us that as adolescents grow and develop, the drug-taking behavior is maintained. In some cases, the drugs used are limited to prescription and over-the-counter substances. In other cases, teen-agers expand into use of wider variety of substances with increased risk.

Not only does drug use affect society, but society affects the use of drugs. Society accepts and uses certain drugs (e.g., caffeine, nicotine, alcohol) on a regular basis; other drugs are growing in use (e.g., marijuana), and the pattern of use of still other drugs (e.g., cocaine) is changing. Oakley Ray, the author of *Drugs, Society and Human Behavior*, points out that drug-taking behavior can be understood and modified.[1]

Drug use in American society should be understood for what it is, not for what it is perceived to be. We must consider the range of drugs (over-the-counter, prescription, illegal street drugs, and alcohol), the various reasons

[1] Ray, O. *Drugs, Society and Human Behavior*, 3rd ed. St. Louis: C.W. Mosby Company, 1983.

for use, and the types of persons who are taking drugs. Alan Cohen suggests that drug use has become a majority phenomenon that is not limited to the young. He further writes that "we must realize that our chemical culture has produced an atmosphere" that leads to use of drugs in American society.[2]

It is extremely important that drug-taking among youth be studied for types of substances used, number of adolescents using them, age of users, and patterns of use. A distinction and clarification between ever-used and used-in-the-past-month must be made. A positive response to ever-used concerning a particular drug might indicate a one-time, experimental use; however, used-in-the-past-month would more probably identify the percentage of young people who are taking drugs on a regular basis. The use of ten classes of drugs by 12- to 17-year-olds in 1982 is summarized as follows:[3]

	Ever Used	Used in Past Month
Marijuana	26.7%	11.5%
Hallucinogens	5.2%	1.4%
Cocaine	6.5%	1.6%
Heroin	less than .5%	less than .5%
Stimulants	6.7%	2.6%
Sedatives	5.8%	1.3%
Tranquilizers	4.9%	.9%
Analgesics	4.2%	.7%
Cigarettes	49.5%	14.7%

[2] Cohen, A.Y. "The Journey Beyond Trips: Alternatives to Drugs." *Journal of Psychedelic Drugs*, 3 (2), pp. 16–21, 1971.

[3] Miller, J.D., Cisin, I.H., Gardner-Keaton, H., Harrell, A.V., Wirtz, P.W., Abelson, H.I., and Fishburne, P.M. *National Survey on Drug Abuse: Main Findings 1982*. Rockville, MD: National Institute on Drug Abuse, 1982.

The statistics indicate that drugs are available and that drug use is occurring in upper elementary school, junior high school, and high school. It is also apparent that a wide variety of substances are being used regularly by some young people. Alcohol is the most prevalent drug used in the past month, as well as ever having been used. Cigarettes are second in both categories, followed by marijuana. The fact that marijuana is illegal and yet obviously obtainable indicates that 12- to 17-year-olds are exposed to illegal substances. The cocaine figures (6.5% ever used and 1.6% used in the past month) may be misleading, since "crack" was not part of the drug scene when the studies were conducted. However, the presence of cocaine and "crack" must be noted. In addition, it is clear that stimulants, sedatives, hallucinogens, tranquilizers, and analgesics have been tried by a small percentage of those surveyed and are still used by an even smaller percentage. The lowest figure is for heroin; less than 1/2 of 1% of the group responded positively for both categories.

Since most high school seniors are age 18 or 19, they are not included in the data provided in the study. However, there are significant reasons to discuss them separately. High school seniors have reachd the end of a developmental stage and are about to complete their public education and make life choices. Some will attend college, others will join the military or the work force, some will move to independent living quarters, marry. Knowledge of this population's use of drugs is particularly helpful to identify trends in younger students as well as future trends in the older population.

Significant findings related to the present use of drugs and trends in use by high school seniors have been identified. A nationwide study of 16,300 high school seniors in 1983 found the following:[4]

	Ever Used	Used in Past Month
Marijuana	57.0%	27.0%
Hallucinogens	11.9%	2.8%
Cocaine	16.2%	4.9%
Heroin	1.2%	0.2%
Stimulants	35.4%	12.4%
Sedatives	14.4%	3.0%
Tranquilizers	13.3%	2.5%
Cigarettes	70.6%	30.3%
Alcohol	92.6%	69.4%

Alcohol, though not legally available for purchase by high school seniors in most states, remains the most used drug, with cigarettes ranking second. Illicit drug use at some time is reported by nearly two thirds of all seniors (63%), though a substantial proportion indicate that the substance used was marijuana. Marijuana is the most widely used illicit drug, with 57% of respondents reporting some use in a lifetime; stimulants are second (35.4%). The used-in-the-past-month category has significantly lower percentage for all types of drugs. The major differences between the two categories seem to support the concept that some drug use is experimental and not maintained as a pattern.

The class of 1983 reported high levels of drug use, described by Johnston as probably reflecting "the highest levels of illicit drug use to be found in any industrialized

[4] Johnston, L.P., O'Malley, P.M., and Bachman, J.G. *Drugs and the American High School Students*, 1975–1983. Rockville, MD: National Institute on Drug Abuse, 1984.

nation in the world." However, the 1983 figures indicate a decline in overall illicit drug use. Compared to the class of 1979 statistics for ever-used, the decline is apparent for marijuana, hallucinogens, tranquilizers, and cigarettes. Increased use of stimulants seems to have occurred, with 24.2% reporting use in 1979 and 35.4% in 1983. A slight increase in reported use of cocaine is noted, from 15.4% in 1979 to 16.2% in 1983. However, the use of "crack," an extremely recent phenomenon, was not a question in the studies conducted in 1979 and 1983. Similar levels of use in 1979 and 1983 were identified for heroin, sedatives, and alcohol.

Daily use of drugs was also surveyed, showing that marijuana was used daily or near daily by 5.5% of high school seniors in 1983; daily use in 1979 was reported at 10.3%. Alcohol was used daily by 5.5% in 1983 and 6.9% in 1979. The impact on health and safety of daily use of drugs indicates reason for concern, as does the finding that approximately 41% of the high school seniors in both 1979 and 1983 reported that they had consumed five or more drinks on at least one occasion in the past two weeks. This level of consumption would result in intoxication for many individuals. The danger and risks related to intoxication impact on the individual and on others. Automobile fatalities, accidents (falls), and antisocial behavior are three visible consequences of intoxication. Other aspects are less visible but also create problems in the individual's life and that of his/her family and friends.

The drug use of two other populations should be briefly described to complete the picture of drug use in American society. The young adult group, age 18 to 25, and the older adult group of 26 and over were both studied by

J.D. Miller and colleagues.[6] Some 94.6% of young adults reported having used alcohol and 67.9% indicated use in the past month; in the older adult category, 88.2% reported ever using and 56.7% noted current use of alcohol. Marijuana use seems to have been prevalent in all age groups, classes, and socioeconomic levels.[7] In Miller's study in 1982, 64.1% of young adults (18 to 25) indicated that they had tried marijuana, and 27.4% reported use in the last month.

Though these figures clearly indicate marijuana use in the 18- to 25-year-old population, they are somewhat lower than in previous years. The older adult group (26 and older) shows a different pattern: Prevalence of marijuana use increased between 1979 and 1982, and current use maintained the pattern. It appears that the group who began using marijuana as teen-agers are growing up and some of them are continuing their pattern of use.

Cocaine use increased steadily in the young adult population in the 1970's: 13.4% in 1976, 27.5% in 1979. However, in 1982 it remained close to the 1979 level, with 28.3% indicating ever having used cocaine. The use of cocaine in the past month (6.8%) in 1982 is a little lower than the 9.3% of 1979. The older population also has an ever-used cocaine group: 2.6% in 1977, 4.3% in 1979, and 8.5% in 1982; use in the past month of 1.2% compares to 0.9% for the same population in 1979. Lifetime prevalence of heroin use among the young adult population

[6] Miller, J.D., Cisin, I.H., Gardner-Keaton, H., Harrell, A.V., Wirtz, P.W., Abelson, H.I., and Fishburne, P.M. *National Survey on Drug Abuse: Main Findings 1982*. Rockville, MD: National Institute on Drug Abuse, 1982.

[7] Hafen, B., and Frandsen, K.J. *Marijuana: Facts, Figures and Information for the 1980's*. Center City, MN: Hazelden, 1980.

decreased from 3.6% in 1977 to 3.5% in 1979 to 1.2% in 1982 (1982); the older adult population seems to have a stable rate of 0.8% in 1977, 1.0% in 1979, and 1.1% in 1982. In Miller's study, nonmedical use of stimulants, sedatives, tranquilizers, and analgesics in the young adult population in 1982 is close to the 1979 figures; when the use of all four substances is combined in a single index, 29.5% is found for 1979 and 28.4% for 1982. The older population indicates a lower ever-used rate of 9.2% in 1979 and 8.8% in 1982 for nonmedical use of stimulants, sedatives, tranquilizers, and analgesics.

Cigarette use also has decreased somewhat for both young adults and older adults; 76.9% of the young adults and 78.7% of the older adults report ever having smoked cigarettes. The current percentages are considerably lower: 39.5% of young adults and 34.6% of older adults in 1982.

When one looks for meaning in the numbers presented on rates of use, trends appear. Some of these trends are positive for society, and others provide cause for alarm.

Reviewing the information on drinking, it is clear that alcohol is part of our society and has been consumed by all ages studied: 65.2% of the 12- to 17-year-olds, 92.6% of the high school seniors, 94.6% of the young adults, and 88.2% of the older adults. Though use in the last month is substantially lower for all age groups, it is clear that a majority of Americans use alcohol on a regular basis: 26.9% of the 12- to 17-year-olds, 69.4% of the high school seniors, 67.9% of the young adults, and 56.7% of the older adults. It s important that we remain aware of alcohol use and its impact on the population. Informational programs should be targeted at all ages to help individuals consider their use of alcohol in the context of their lives. Responsibility for use of alcohol appropriately rests on the individual; society can foster healthy attitudes by dealing with alcohol problems and by supporting positive messages relating to alcohol use.

Marijuana use appears to be related to age, with 26.7% of the 12- to 17-year-olds indicating ever having used it, 57.0% of the high school seniors, and 64.1% of the young adults. Use in the past month for the various ages is as follows: 11.5% for 12- to 17-year-olds, 27.0% for high school seniors, and 27.4% for young adults. Also, as was mentioned earlier, the prevalence of marijuana use has been increasing in the older adult population. Our society must focus on the use of marijuana, the personal and societal problems caused by use, and the issues related to use. The statistics make it clear that marijuana is available, yet little attention is currently paid to marijuana. We must continue to research the impact of this substance on the body, deal with the fact that it is available to both youthful and older populations, provide information, and implement strategies to deal with its use. A major problem to be dealt with is the mixing of alcohol and marijuana. Both substances may be available at a party, and the reasons for not combining them should be made clear. Quite simply, we must confront the issue of marijuana in America. Pretending that it is gone from the scene or is no longer a concern is a disservice to all of us.

Use of cocaine is apparent throughout all the ages reviewed: 6.5% of the 12- to 17-years-olds studied, 16.2% of the high school seniors, 28.3% of the young adults, and 8.5% of the older adults. The significance of these numbers lies in the fact that such percentages of our population have tried cocaine. Though the number who indicate use in the past month is much lower (1.6% of the 12- to 17-year-olds, 4.9% of the high school seniors, 6.8%

of the young adults, and 1.2% of the older adults), it is clear that cocaine use is a growing problem.

The U.S. has been alerted, frightened, and motivated to deal with cocaine by the increasingly widespread use of "crack," a derivative of cocaine. Though percentages of use are not available for crack, it seems clear that it is growing in use, especially among the youthful population. Dealing with this phenomenon will take time and effort combined with creativity and perseverance. It is not enough to try to close the routes by which cocaine enters the country. We must reduce the numbers of individuals who are willing to try this substance and endanger their health, well-being, and quality of life.

The use of sedatives and tranquilizers needs to be considered. Nonmedical use definitely increases with age. When statistics for these substances are combined, about 5% to 6% of the 12- to 17-year-olds have tried them, 13% to 14% of the high school seniors, 25% to 30% of young adults, and close to 10% of the older adults. This suggests that some people are using drugs to stay calm and to slow down. Even greater numbers are using stimulants to keep going; the number of young people who had tried them and who used them regularly is distressing. In the 12- to 17-year-old group, 6.7% had used them and 2.6% in the last month; in the high school senior group, 35.4% had used them and 12.4% in the last month.

A positive trend is apparent in cigarette smoking. Of the 49.5% of the 12- to 17-year-olds who ever smoked, 14.7% smoked in the last month; and of the 70.6% of high school seniors who ever smoked, 30.3% smoked in the last month. Decreases in smoking of young adults and older adults are also evident. Society has indeed begun to deal with motivating people to stop smoking, and the efforts are meeting with success.

The U.S. needs to deal with the issue of drugs in a clear, open, and honest fashion for citizens of all ages. Information needs to be incorporated into school programs, youth groups, church centers, and industry efforts. The public should be helped to clarify their feelings about drugs and to make responsible decisions regarding use of drugs.

Appendix

SUGGESTED READINGS

The following bibliography is coded for audience in the lefthand margin by "A" designating adults (parents, teachers, etc.) and by "S" indicating students.

A   Ackerman, R.J. *Children of Alcoholics: A Guidebook for Educators, Therapists, and Parents.* Holmes Beach, FL: Learning Publications, 1983.

S   Addiction Research Foundation. *Coffee, Tea and Me.* Toronto: Addiction Research Foundation, 1980.

S   Addiction Research Foundation. *Facts About Alcohol,* rev. ed. Toronto: Addiction Research Foundation, 1980.

A   Al-Anon Family Group Headquarters. *Al-Anon Faces Alcoholism,* 2d ed. New York: Al-Anon Family Group Headquarters, Inc., 1984.

S   Al-Anon Family Group Headquarters. *Facts About Alateen.* New York: Al-Anon Family Group Headquarters, Inc., 1979.

S   Al-Anon Family Group Headquarters. *What's Drunk, Mama?* New York: Al-Anon Family Group Headquarters, Inc., 1977.

S   Al-Anon Family Group Headquarters. *Youth and the Alcoholic Parent.* New York: Al-Anon Family Group Headquarters, Inc., 1979.

A,S   *Alcohol: A Family Affair.* A PTA pamphlet. Washington, D.C.: National Clearinghouse for Alcohol Information, 1975.

A   Alcoholics Anonymous. *44 Questions.* New York: Alcoholics Anonymous World Services, n.d.

A   CASPAR Alcohol Education Program and Somerville Public School Faculty Team. *Decisions About Drinking: A Sequential Alcohol Education Curriculum for Grades 3–12.* Somerville, Mass: CASPAR Alcohol Education Project, 1978.

A,S   Chafetz, M., M.D. *Why Drinking Can Be Good for You.* New York: Stein and Day, 1977.

A   Cohen, S. *The Substance Abuse Problems.* New York: The Haworth Press, 1981.

A   Deutsch, C. *Broken Bottles, Broken Dreams: Understanding and Helping the Children of Alcoholics.* Safety Research and Education Project. New York: Teachers College, Columbia University, 1982.

S   Education Commission of the States. *What Students Should Know About Drinking and Pregnancy.* Denver: Education Commission of the States, 1980.

A,S   Evans, D.G. *Kids, Drugs and the Law.* Center City, MN: Hazelden, 1985.

    Fensterheim, H., and Baer, J. *Don't Say Yes When You Want to Say No.* Center City, MN: Hazelden, 1978.

A   Finn, P., and O'Gorman, P.A. *Teaching About Alcohol: Concepts, Methods and Classroom Activities.* Boston: Allen and Bacon, 1981.

A   Fornaciari, S. *How to Talk to Kids About Drugs.* Bethesda: Potomac Press, 1980.

A   Gitlow, S.E., and Peyser, H.S., eds. *Alcoholism: A Practical Treatment Guide.* New York: Grune and Stratton, 1980.

A   Gomberg, E., White, H.R., and Carpenter, J.A., eds. *Alcohol, Science and Society Revisited.*

New Brunswick, NJ: Rutgers Center of Alcohol Studies, 1982.

A   Goodman, J., Reed, D., and Simon, S. *Health Education: The Search for Values.* New York: Prentice-Hall, 1977.

A,S Goodwin, D.W. *Alcoholism: The Facts.* New York: Oxford University Press, 1981.

S   Gordon, Sol. *You.* New York: Quadrangle—The New York Times Book Co., 1975.

A   Griffin, T., and Svendsen, R. *The Student Assistance Program: How It Works,* rev. ed. Center City, MN: Hazelden, 1986.

A   Hafen, B.Q., and Frandsen, K.J. *Drug and Alcohol Emergencies.* Center City, MN: Hazelden, 1980.

A   *How to Talk to Your Teenager About Drinking and Driving.* Washington, D.C.: U.S. National Highway Traffic Safety Administration, in cooperation with the National Congress of Parents and Teachers, 1975.

A   Hyman, M.M., Zimmermann, M.A., Gurioli, C., and Helrich, A. *Drinkers, Drinking and Alcohol-Related Mortality and Hospitalizations: A Statistical Compendium.* New Brunswick, NJ: Rutgers Center of Alcohol Studies, 1980.

S   Irwin, S. *Drugs of Abuse: An Introduction to Their Actions and Potential Hazards.* Phoenix: D.I.N. Publications, 1986.

A   Johnson, V.E. *Intervention: How to Help Someone Who Doesn't Want Help.* Minneapolis: Johnson Institute Books, 1986.

S   ———. *Why Do They Have to Suffer So Long?* Center City, MN: Hazelden, 1980.

A   Jones, K.L., Shainberg, L.W., and Byer, C.O. *Drugs and Alcohol.* New York: Harper and Row, Publishers, 1979.

A   Keller, M. *The Definition of Alcoholism.* New Brunswick, N.J.: Rutgers Center of Alcohol Studies, 1960.

A,S Keller, M., McCormick, M., and Efron, V. *A Dictionary of Words About Alcohol.* New Brunswick, NJ: Rutgers Center of Alcohol Studies, 1982.

A,S Kinney, J., and Leaton, G. *Loosening the Grip: A Handbook of Alcohol Information.* St. Louis: C.V. Mosby Company, 1983.

A,S Kurtz, E. *Not-God: A History of Alcoholics Anonymous.* Center City, MN: Hazelden, 1979.

A,S Lender, M.E., and Martin, J.K. *Drinking in America: A History.* New York: The Free Press, 1982.

S Mann, M. *Marty Mann Answers Your Questions About Drinking and Alcoholism.* New York: Holt, Rinehart & Winston, 1970.

A Manning, W.O., and Vinton, J. *Harmfully Involved.* Center City, MN: Hazelden, 1980.

A McCarthy, B.G., ed. *Alcohol Education for Classroom and Community: A Source Book for Educators.* New York: McGraw-Hill, 1964.

A Milgram, G.G. "Alcohol," in *Teaching About Drugs: A Curriculum Guide, K-12.* Kent, OH: American School Health Association, 1985.

S ———. *What Is Alcohol and Why Do People Drink?* New Brunswick, NJ: Rutgers Center of Alcohol Studies, 1975.

A ———. *What, When and How to Talk to Children About Alcohol and Other Drugs: A Guide for Parents.* Center City, MN: Hazelden, 1983.

A Milgram, G.G., and Griffin, T. *What, When, and How to Talk to Students About Alcohol and Other Drugs: A Guide for Teachers.* Center City, MN: Hazelden, 1986.

A,S Narcotics Anonymous. *Narcotics Anonymous.* Sun Valley, CA: Narcotics Anonymous World Service Office, Inc., 1982.

A O'Gorman, P.A., Stringfield, R.N., and Smith, E., eds. *Defining Adolescent Alcohol Use: Implications*

Toward a Definition of Adolescent Alcoholism. New York: National Council on Alcoholism, Inc., 1977.

A,S Pursch, J.A. *Dear Doc* ... Minneapolis: CompCare Publications, 1979.

A Ray, O. *Drugs, Society and Human Behavior.* St. Louis: C.V. Mosby Company, 1983.

A Roberts, C., and Mooney, C. *Here's Looking at You: A Teacher's Guide for Alcohol Education,* rev. ed. Seattle: Comprehensive Health Education Foundation, 1980.

A Rosett, H.L., and Weiner, L. *Alcohol and the Fetus: A Clinical Perspective.* New York: Oxford University Press, 1984.

A Russell, R. *The Last Bell Is Ringing.* Chicago: Midwestern Area Alcohol Education and Training Program, Inc., 1976.

A ———. *What Shall We Teach the Young About Drinking?,* rev. ed. New Brunswick, NJ: Rutgers Center of Alcohol Studies, 1986.

A Russell, Robert D. *Health Education.* Washington, D.C.: National Education Association, 1975.

A,S Silverstein, A. and V. *Alcoholism.* Philadelphia: Lippincott, 1975.

A Strachan, J.G. *Alcoholism: Treatable Illness, An Update for the 80's.* Center City, MN: Hazelden, 1982.

A,S U.S. Department of Health and Human Services. *Fifth Special Report to the U.S. Congress on Alcohol and Health.* Rockville, MD: National Institute on Alcohol Abuse and Alcoholism, 1983.

A,S Wegscheider, S. *The Family Trap ... No One Escapes from a Chemically Dependent Family.* Minneapolis: The Johnson Institute, 1978.

A Woititz, J.G. *Adult Children of Alcoholics.* Hollywood, FL: Health Communications, Inc., 1983.

Resources for Additional Information

Addiction Research Foundation
33 Russell Street
Toronto, Ontario M5S 2Sl, Canada

Al-Anon Family Group Headquarters, Inc.
P.O. Box 182
Madison Square Garden Station
New York, NY 10159–0182

Alateen
P.O. Box 182
Madison Square Garden Station
New York, NY 10159–0182

Alcohol and Drug Problems Association of North America, Inc.
444 North Capitol Street, NW
Washington, DC 20001

Alcoholics Anonymous World Services, Inc.
468 Park Avenue South
New York, NY 10016

American Medical Association
535 Dearborn Street
Chicago, IL 60610

Distilled Spirits Council of the United States (DISCUS)
1250 Eye Street, NW
Washington, DC 20005

National Clearinghouse for Alcohol Information
P.O. Box 2345
Rockville, MD 20852

National Congress of Parents and Teachers
Program Department
700 North Rush Street
Chicago, IL 60611

National Council on Alcoholism, Inc.
12 West 21st Street
New York, NY 10017

National Institute on Alcohol Abuse and Alcoholism
5600 Fishers Lane
Rockville, MD 20582

North Conway Institute
14 Beacon Street
Boston, MA 02108

Publications Division
Rutgers Center of Alcohol Studies
Rutgers—The State University
New Brunswick, NJ 08903

The Division of Alcoholism, the Department of Education, the
State Department of Mental Health, and the State Safety
Councils of each state also may have alcohol information
available for distribution.

Glossary

AA: abbreviation for Alcoholics Anonymous.

Abstinence: refraining from drinking alcoholic beverages.

Abuse: to use wrongly or improperly; misuse.

Acetaldehyde: substance formed in the liver during the oxidation of ethyl alcohol. It is then combined with oxygen in any living tissue to produce acetic acid.

Acetic acid: substance formed by the union of oxygen and acetaldehyde in any tissue of the body. Acetic acid is then oxidized to produce water and carbon dioxide.

Addiction: dependence on a substance, which the addict will obtain and use by any means. Alcohol addiction is the loss of control over drinking.

Al-Anon: group of spouses or relatives of alcoholics. They meet to discuss the problems of alcoholism as well as constructive ways to help the alcoholic.

Alateen: organization of teen-age children of alcoholics. They meet to obtain understanding of the disease alcoholism and for mutual support in facing the problem of an alcoholic parent.

Alcohol: unless otherwise stated, this refers to ethyl alcohol, which is a colorless, odorless, and volatile liquid. It is produced by fermentation of certain carbohydrates such as grains, molasses, or sugar. It is used in beverages, medicines, lotions, and also as a solvent.

Alcoholic: a person suffering from the disease of alcoholism who has lost control of his drinking.

Alcoholics Anonymous: a fellowship of people who admit that they are powerless to control their drinking and who desire to stop drinking entirely.

Alcoholism: disease characterized by a dependence on alcohol and loss of control of the use of alcohol.

Alcohols: compounds composed of carbon, hydrogen, and oxygen. They are amyl, butyl, ethyl, methyl, and propyl.

Ale: alcoholic beverage obtained by the fermentation of grain.

Amyl alcohol: colorless and sharp-smelling alcohol derived mainly from fusel oil, though it can be manufactured synthetically.

Antabuse: drug often used in the medical treatment of alcoholics. It causes a physical reaction such as nausea if alcohol is consumed while the Antabuse is still in effect.

Beer: alcoholic beverage obtained by the fermentation of barley malt and flavored with hops. Beer generally contains between 3 and 6 percent alcohol by volume.

Beriberi: illness due to a deficiency of vitamin B_1, sometimes associated with alcoholism.

Beverage alcohol: generally alcoholic beverages or alcohol in various beverages.

Blackout: loss of memory of events that occurred during a drinking session or immediately thereafter.

Blood Alcohol Concentration (BAC): percentage of alcohol present in a person's blood.

Brewing: fermentation process of making beer.

Butyl alcohol: often called butanol. It is used as a solvent and also in lacquer, insect sprays, and paints for application over asphalt.

Carbonation: bubbles of carbon dioxide in drinks. The process may occur naturally or may be produced synthetically.

Cirrhosis of the liver: disease of the liver often associated with alcoholism. Liver function, blood circulation, and flow of bile are impaired.

Cocktail: drink composed of a distilled beverage or wine and another ingredient. It is usually served chilled or over ice.

Concentration of alcohol: percentage of alcohol in a beverage.

Beer contains between 3 and 6 percent alcohol, whereas wine contains between 5 and 20 percent, and distilled beverages contain between 40 and 50 percent.

Delirium tremens: temporary mental condition associated with alcoholism. In this state, the person is disoriented and confused and often has hallucinations.

Denatured alcohol: alcohol combined with a poison such as formaldehyde to make it unfit for human consumption.

Depressant: substance that reduces the functions of the central nervous system.

Distillation: process of heating a fermented beverage and allowing the alcohol to escape as a gas. The alcohol gas is recaptured and cooled, yielding a distilled beverage.

Drinker: person who consumes alcoholic beverages.

Drinking: consuming alcoholic beverages.

Drinking behavior: conduct of a drinker.

Driving While Intoxicated (DWI): In most states a person is considered to be driving while intoxicated if the BAC is .10 percent; called Driving Under the Influence (DUI) in some areas.

Drug: any substance other than a food which, when introduced into the body, alters the body or its functions.

Drunk: state of being severely affected by alcohol; that is, intoxicated or inebriated.

Eighteenth Amendment: amendment to the United States Constitution passed in 1917 and taking effect in 1920. It prohibited the manufacture, sale, and transportation of intoxicating liquors in the United States.

Ethyl alcohol: that form of alcohol present in beer, wines, and liquors and called simply alcohol. When full strength, it is used as a solvent and in the manufacture of paint, dyes, and varnishes.

Fermentation: process that produces ethyl alcohol. Yeast is added to glucose sugar, yielding ethyl alcohol and carbon dioxide.

Fetal Alcohol Syndrome (FAS): Adverse effects on the fetus resulting from consumption of large amounts of alcohol during pregnancy. Abnormalities characteristic of FAS are low birth weight, prenatal or postnatal retardation of growth, cranial facial disorders, limb disorders; other abnormalities (cardiac, genital, ear) are present. Central nervous system damage manifested by mental retardation is also a characteristic of the syndrome.

Fortification: addition of a distilled beverage to a wine to increase the alcohol content.

Halfway House: facility for alcoholics that bridges the gap between an institution and a return to family and community life. The members sleep and eat at the Halfway House and go into the community to work.

Hallucinations: often associated with alcoholism and occurring as a withdrawal symptom. The person hears voices and occasionally sees what is not there.

Hangover: effects of having consumed an excess of alcoholic beverages. These effects are fatigue, headache, nausea, and feelings of guilt and depression.

High: state of being affected by alcohol. This is characterized by gaiety, impaired movement, thick speech, and drowsiness.

Highball: a drink composed of a distilled liquor, such as whisky or rum, mixed with water, soda, ginger ale, etc., served with ice in a tall glass.

Inebriation: state of being intoxicated.

Intoxicating beverage: beverage containing alcohol.

Intoxication: state of drunkenness, produced by excessive use of toxic drugs.

Korsakoff's psychosis: mental disorder associated with alcoholism. The main characteristic is its effect on memory.

Liquor: alcoholic beverage. The word liquor often is used to refer only to distilled beverages.

Marijuana: Mexican name, of unknown origin, of the plant *Cannabis sativa* or parts of it.

Medicinal: having healing qualities.

Methyl alcohol: often called wood alcohol. Used as a solvent, antifreeze, and in varnishes and paint removers. It is a poison if consumed and may result in blindness or death.

Non-beverage alcohol: alcohol that is not intended for drinking.

Oxidation of alcohol: bodily process of converting alcohol to carbon dioxide and water. This process is accompanied by the release of heat and energy.

Pellagra: condition caused by a deficiency of vitamin B (nicotinic acid) in the body. It is often associated with alcoholism and is generally characterized by rough skin, diarrhea, and a sore mouth.

Phases of alcoholism: stages of the progressive disease of alcoholism. They are the warning stage, the preliminary stage, the crucial stage, and the chronic stage.

Problem drinker: excessive drinker whose drinking causes problems for himself and others.

Prohibition: forbidding by law of the sale, manufacture, and transportation of intoxicating beverages. Prohibition was in effect in the United States between 1920 and 1933.

Proof: measure of amount of alcohol present in distilled beverages. One hundred proof means that the beverage contains 50 percent alcohol by volume.

Propyl alcohol: often called propanol. Derived mainly from petroleum gases. It can also be produced synthetically. Propyl alcohol is mainly used as a solvent, though it is also used in rubbing alcohol and as a lacquer thinner.

Psychoses: mental disorders often associated with alcoholism. Victims of psychoses are unable to judge between what is real and what is unreal. Alcoholic psychoses include delirium tremens, hallucinosis, Korsakoff's psychosis, and Wernicke's disease.

Rehabilitation: bringing an alcoholic to a condition of good physical health with the ability to live again in society.

Social drinking: use of alcoholic beverages in social situations such as get-togethers and parties.

Still: device for distillation.

Synergism: effect of a combination of drugs which, when taken simultaneously, have an effect greater than the sum of the same drugs when taken separately.

Twenty-first Amendment: amendment to the Constitution of the United States in 1933. This amendment repealed Prohibition.

Wernicke's disease: condition associated with alcoholism. It is characterized by unclear consciousness, disorientation, weakness of eye muscles, and difficulty in comprehension.

Whisky: distilled beverage. This includes rye, scotch, and bourbon.

Wine: fermented beverage from fruit, plants, or vegetables.

Withdrawal: abstention from drugs to which one is habituated or addicted; the term also denotes the symptoms of such withdrawal.

Woman's Christian Temperance Union (W.C.T.U.): American women's organization founded in 1874 to spread the principle of total abstinence from alcoholic beverages. This organization sought the abolishment of the manufacture and sale of alcoholic beverages.

Index

problem, xx, 47, 54, 83–84,
91, 92, 94, 100
reasons for, 46–47, 50–51,
56–57, 83
responsible, xvii, 47, 71
social, 49
spacing, 73
teen-age, xiii, xv, 43–58
times of, 47, 84
without getting drunk, 76–77
driving
while impaired, 77
while intoxicated, 2, 54, 58,
74, 76, 77
drug
alcohol as, xiii, xvi, xviii, 19,
21–22, 86, 87
use, by age groups, 107–118
drugs
hard, xvi, 21, 108, 109, 112
and alcohol, 55
legal, xiii, 19, 21–22
over-the-counter, 1, 107, 109
prescription, 1, 19, 107–109
*Drugs, Society and Human
Behavior*, 109
drunk, xv, 75–76
dry wine, 29

E
education, alcohol, xiii-xiv,
xvii, xviii, xix
effects on body, of alcohol,
59–74
Eighteenth Amendment, 24, 25
elimination, of alcohol, 68,
80–81,
emotions
bottling up, 102
intensified, 65
ethyl alcohol (ethanol), 17, 18
exercises, values clarification,
5–16, 40
exhilaration, 63, 66, 69

expectations, of drinker, 49, 59,
62–63, 78
experience
with alcohol, 59, 78–79
lack of, 55, 78
with drugs, 109

F
family
feelings about alcohol, xix, 4
illness, alcoholism as, 99–103
feelings
about alcohol, xv
clarifying, xix, 44, 105
about use and nonuse,
39–41, 48
guilt, 79, 87, 99–100, 101,
102
fermentation, 27–31, 32
food
alcohol as, 18–19
and effects of alcohol, 49, 59,
62, 78
serving, with drinks, 72–73
fortified wine, 30
fruits, 27, 34, 35, 36

G
gin, 33, 34
grapes, 28–29, 35
gratification, instant, 1–2

H
halfway house, 96–97
hallucinogens, 110, 111, 112,
113
hangover, 21, 65, 75, 79, 80, 81
health, 105
effects of alcohol on, 69–70
neglect of, 100
*Health Education: The Search
for Values*, 3
heavy drinking, 45–46, 51, 53,
55